BBC MUSIC GUIDES

353-2
31

PURCELL

BBC MUSIC GUIDES

Bach Cantatas J. A. WESTRUP
Bach Organ Music PETER WILLIAMS
Bartók Chamber Music STEPHEN WALSH
Bartók Orchestral Music JOHN MCCABE
Beethoven Concertos and Overtures ROGER FISKE
Beethoven Piano Sonatas DENIS MATTHEWS
Beethoven String Quartets BASIL LAM
Beethoven Symphonies ROBERT SIMPSON
Berlioz Orchestral Music HUGH MACDONALD
Brahms Chamber Music IVOR KEYS
Brahms Piano Music DENIS MATTHEWS
Brahms Orchestral Music JOHN HORTON
Brahms Songs ERIC SAMS
Bruckner Symphonies PHILIP BARFORD
Couperin DAVID TUNLEY
Debussy Orchestral Music DAVID COX
Debussy Piano Music FRANK DAWES
Dvořák Symphonies and Concertos ROBERT LAYTON
Elgar Orchestral Music MICHAEL KENNEDY
Falla RONALD CRICHTON
Handel Concertos STANLEY SADIE
Haydn String Quartets ROSEMARY HUGHES
Haydn Symphonies H. C. ROBBINS LANDON
Mahler Symphonies and Songs PHILIP BARFORD
Mendelssohn Chamber Music JOHN HORTON
Monteverdi Church Music DENIS ARNOLD
Monteverdi Madrigals DENIS ARNOLD
Mozart Chamber Music A. HYATT KING
Mozart Piano Concertos PHILIP RADCLIFFE
Mozart Serenades, Divertimenti and Dances ERIK SMITH
Mozart Wind and String Concertos A. HYATT KING
Rachmaninov Orchestral Music PATRICK PIGGOTT
Ravel Orchestral Music LAURENCE DAVIES
Schoenberg Chamber Music ARNOLD WHITTALL
Schubert Chamber Music J. A. WESTRUP
Schubert Piano Sonatas PHILIP RADCLIFFE
Schubert Songs MAURICE J. E. BROWN
Schubert Symphonies MAURICE J. E. BROWN
Schumann Orchestral Music HANS GAL
Schumann Piano Music JOAN CHISSELL
Schumann Songs ASTRA DESMOND
Shostakovich Symphonies HUGH OTTAWAY
Tchaikovsky Ballet Music JOHN WARRACK
Tchaikovsky Symphonies and Concertos JOHN WARRACK
The Trio Sonata CHRISTOPHER HOGWOOD
Vaughan Williams Symphonies HUGH OTTAWAY
Vivaldi MICHAEL TALBOT
Hugo Wolf Songs MOSCO CARNER

BBC MUSIC GUIDES

Purcell

ARTHUR HUTCHINGS

BRITISH BROADCASTING CORPORATION

Contents

Published by the
British Broadcasting Corporation
35 Marylebone High Street
London W1M 4AA

ISBN 0 563 17184 7

First published 1982

Filmset in Great Britain by
August Filmsetting, Warrington, Cheshire
Printed in England by Hollen Street Press, Slough, Berks

The dates 1659–95 are easy to remember. They show that Henry Purcell, whom British musicians regard as their most talented forbear, lived only one more year than Mozart and five longer than Schubert. They also show his and our good fortune, for within a few months of his birth the monarchy and established Church were restored in England, and with them a demand for two kinds of public music that had been out of official commission when the puritan government closed the theatres and outlawed Anglican worship. Music was then classified in Western countries according to the places in which it sounded – church, theatre, the home. During the public repression of the first two the third, chamber music, was outstandingly cultivated, and needed only its late harvest from Purcell to reach a glory unparalleled in the same forms and with the same instruments from composers overseas.

The most admirable English chamber music before Purcell's is found in the consorts for viols or recorders, with or without keyboard instruments, by Gibbons, Jenkins, Locke and William Lawes (the second- and third-mentioned of these lived to welcome the Restoration). But 'chamber music' designated any works purveyed for pleasure in 'the residences of princes and noblemen'.[1] It therefore included a sound which before Purcell's time had been heard by only a few favoured Englishmen: that made by a large ensemble with bowed string instruments of the type used today. During the king's exile this *orchestra* (then a word newly applied to a body of musicians) was ascendant in France and in German-speaking courts whose princelings envied Louis XIV and his *grande bande*. Although violins had been used at the funeral of Elizabeth I (1603) and James I (1635), visitors were at first shocked to hear them in a larger force at 'the first time of change' (1662) in the Chapel Royal.

The court establishment already included singers, lutenists and performers on viols, wind and keyboard instruments, but Charles II preferred the new band modelled on the *Vingt-quatre violons du Roi* 'as being more brisk and airy'[2] or, as we should say, 'rhythmically precise and catchy-tuneful'. It attended at banquets and court functions, ministering to pleasure rather than con-

[1] Dr Charles Burney (1726–1814) in Rees' *Cyclopaedia* (*c.* 1800).
[2] Anthony Wood (1632–95), *Life and Times*, ed. Andrew Clarke, 5 vols, Oxford 1891, Vol. I, p. 212.

templation. Pepys, Evelyn and Wood, though men of pleasure, evidently regarded as foreign – geographically and metaphorically – the belief that in the *teatrum sacrum* such music should not merely prolong the contemplation of words but sound for divine and human pleasure. 'A Consort of 24 violins between every pause, after the French fantastical light way, better suiting a Tavern or Play-house than a Church': Evelyn may have attended upon an occasion when the King wanted to convert others to his relish of the full band, for we have rosters requiring only a quarter of the total to attend the chapel at a time. They were responsible to Thomas Purcell, Henry's father, or to Pelham Humfrey, who had returned after a 'travelling scholarship' to France and Italy and had been among the first batch of boys to be trained for the reopened Chapel Royal.

Brought up among their father's musical friends and relatives in royal service, Henry Purcell and his younger brother, Daniel, became Chapel Royal choristers with scarlet liveries of the kind still used today. Distinctive at the English Reformation had been the establishment of collegiate foundations at cathedrals, royal 'peculiars' (for example, Westminster Abbey or St George's, Windsor) and the universities. A choral foundation included clergy, singing men, organists and a school for the boys. The Continent had no exact parallel, for the resident choirs in England maintained weekday offices. The Imperial Konvict at Vienna, where Haydn and Schubert were educated, took choristers without fees, but the 'Vienna Boys' Choir' and the choir at Regensburg are modern revivals. Apart from the normal school curriculum, our choral foundations expect boys also to practise keyboard and orchestral instruments, and to study harmony and musical design. Charles II's boys were further encouraged to compose works that would be performed during services, for by 'indulging their youthful fancies' the King secured music for his Whitehall chapel in styles he preferred to those of older composers.[1]

[1] The information comes from Tudway, who was among the first Restoration choristers. Between 1715 and 1720 he assembled a valuable collection of cathedral music. Whitehall Palace was ruined by fire in 1698 and pulled down, but Inigo Jones's lovely Banqueting Hall served as the Chapel Royal until closed by Queen Victoria. Thereafter the Chapel Royal, as now, was the Tudor one at St James's Palace. Soon after the Second World War the choir school was closed. Normally the boys (unlike cathedral boys) attend services only on Sundays, and they are better served at schools which have room for science teaching, athletics, and so on. Most

But why comment at length upon·the chorister years of a man who wrote far more secular than sacred music? Because Cooke, Humfrey, Blow, Locke and his other mentors in the royal service had absorbed influences which stimulated his originality while he was still in his teens. He never travelled far from London and would not have gained unique honour at home unless his music disarmed regret that he had not been abroad. We should therefore know the features which flattered the taste of his contemporaries, however naive their supposed connoisseurship. A vocal or instrumental piece with precise rhythms and metrical accents like those of the minuet, gavotte or march, the texture using block harmony more than overlapping strands, was thought to be in 'the French style'. A contrast with 'the English style' may be recognised in Exx. 1 and 2 (overleaf), settings of the same words by Gibbons (d. 1625) and Purcell. At the beginning of 'generations' Purcell has the *saccadé* (jerked) figure, associated with Lully's pompous pieces and much employed by Restoration composers.

The part-writing in broad phrases is made clearer by omitting modern bar lines from Ex. 1, which would be spoilt by accenting the first and third beat of conventional 4/2 rhythm. Sometimes Purcell wrote similar music, yet even in the 'French' Ex. 2 the words take broad phrases and should not be sung with heavy accents after bar lines. We also recognise in Ex. 2 a polyphonist's ability to make all parts melodically interesting – not a Lullian characteristic! Does any other setting of *Magnificat* so effectively make a minor climax on the last syllable of 'For behold from hence-*forth*'? Not only traditional or conservative music was thought to be in 'the English style'. The phrase was more often used to desig-nate textures stiffened by discords – not just the suspensions and passing notes without which counterpoint is weak, but bold dis-cords derived from the invention of parts melodious in themselves but causing clashes with another part; for instance, an F natural against an F sharp. Soon after Purcell's death critics who had sampled the plainer harmonies of Lully and Corelli thought their native textures rough. According to Roger North, Purcell's 'noble set of sonatas' was 'unworthily despised for being clog'd with some-what of an English vein'. Later in the eighteenth century Burney compiled 'a list of Dr Blow's crudities'; he could have made cap-

cathedral choir schools admit other pupils than the singing boys and do not face expansion problems as severe as those in the City of Westminster.

Ex.1   Gibbons

For be-hold from hence forth all gen-er-

-a- -tions shall call me bless- ed

Ex.2   Purcell

For be-hold, be-hold from hence-forth all

gen-er-a-tions shall call me bless-ed

tures from Purcell. Specimens from one movement of one work are shown at Ex. 3. Another 'English' feature, fondness for modulation, is seen in Ex. 4a (overleaf), which is not obviously contrapuntal, yet the contrapuntal clash in Ex. 4b also incurs an effect of modulation.

Ex.3   Purcell: Sonata No. 6

At the beginning of the century Monteverdi and other Italians had used bold turns of harmony in dramatic settings of works; by Purcell's time the Italians had moved towards the suavity and clarity we associate with their violin sonatas and concertos. English musicians may not have recognised that denial of church patronage during the Commonwealth averted interest in a limited expression and technique. (Even Monteverdi observed Palestrinian decorum to please the procurators of St Mark's.) Masques and chamber works for private patrons encouraged enterprise, for the patrons were often connoisseurs and travelled persons. Like their English successors two centuries later, who reacted against Victorian conventions, Purcell's forbears, especially the ruggedly independent Locke, advanced harmonic resource and modulation. We tend to regard some points of their styles, especially those using chromatics, as part of the Purcellian idiom unless we are acquainted with the composers whom Purcell outshone.

Solo declamation, of which plenty was composed in England before the Restoration, was supposedly a feature of 'the Italian style'. In fact English 'recitative musique', which Dryden distinguished from 'songish', was usually more 'songish' than most

Ex.4   Purcell: Four-part Fantasia, No. 1

(a)

(b)   Fantasia, No. 4

Italian recitative; the bass, and therefore the harmony, was more enterprising and might change rapidly for emotional effect when the words did not. Moreover the bar lines were observed as in Lully's *récit*. To modern ears Ex. 5 and Ex. 6 are not particularly Italianate; they are simply worthy of Purcell for adventurous sensitivity to dramatic language. The example from Blow needs the bass to show an almost Fauréan love of modulation.

When Purcell joined the Chapel Royal choir the Master of the

Ex.5   Humfrey: "Hear, O heav'ns"

Ex.6   Blow: Venus and Adonis

Children was still Captain Cooke, a fine singer who – until the first recruited boys were proficient – provided much solo work in anthems. In choruses such instruments as the wooden cornetts might strengthen or replace trebles, but the counter-tenor voice was also useful and remained for some time a favourite for solos in anthems, odes, theatre songs and oratorios. Pepys declared that

Cooke's boys 'could sing anything at sight' including 'Italian songs'. (Purcell's preface to his sonatas regrets that he was not formally taught Italian.) Cooke's flair for juvenile musical intelligence is proved by his first choristers, among whom were Blow, Humfrey, Turner and Wise. He did not 'select' the Purcell boys, whose father and uncle were Gentlemen of the Chapel and held other royal appointments.

Cooke died in 1672 and was replaced by his twenty-five-year-old son-in-law, Humfrey, who might have become an important dramatic composer if he had not died two years later. By then Purcell was fifteen. He had left the choir with the usual grants of money, linen and so forth, to become unpaid assistant to John Hingston as 'keeper, repairer and tuner of the regals, organs, virginals, flutes, recorders and all other wind instruments . . . to his Majesty', with the promise of replacing Hingston and taking the stipend at Hingston's 'death or other avoidance'. How valuable was this appointing of *very* young men to offices of trust and dignity, just when they could exult in exacting and challenging work!

John Blow (not yet Dr Blow) succeeded Humfrey but retained his post of organist of Westminster Abbey. It is known that Purcell's broken voice changed to a bass that could also do well as a so-called counter-tenor, making one suspicious of those who dislike the word 'falsetto'; but under Blow he cannot have been enrolled in the Chapel Royal choir. Nevertheless Blow became his most influential mentor – even more so than Locke, a friend of the Purcell family. Blow's monument in the Abbey calls him 'Master to the famous Mr H. Purcell'. He was ten years older than Purcell, who had reached his most impressionable years. What formal tuition was given? Organ lessons? Counterpoint? The art of integrating extended music? Whatever the answers, Blow resigned his Abbey post in Purcell's favour at Michaelmas 1679 and went back to it when Purcell died. We may doubt the attractive story that this showed abnormal generosity and modesty in recognition of genius. The beneficiary, aged twenty, was not yet 'the famous Mr H. Purcell'. Moreover the Abbey organist was not choirmaster nor, apart from house rent, was he paid more than a singing man. No doubt there was affection and respect between the two musicians but Blow may have shed a burden from an overload. At that time he badly needed time for composition, but both Chapel Royal and Abbey maintained two daily choral services.

Purcell's biography can be read elsewhere since this guide is concerned only with what may immediately have affected his music.[1] We therefore add a summary of facts which explain not only his amazing versatility but the demand that evoked it. Purcell married at the age of twenty-two. Musicians without private means could not maintain a home and family unless they had patrons: church officers, theatre managers, monarchs or music-loving aristocrats. Publication brought no royalties though they spread repute, and payment by publishers was meagre by modern standards. The place and time of Purcell's upbringing, as well as his relatives and friends, enabled him to outdo even Locke or Blow in scooping up appointments, incurring none of the accusations of unscrupulousness attached to Lully. Let the dates of some speak for themselves:

1677 Composer in Ordinary for the royal violins (i.e. orchestra) on the death of Locke
1679 Organist of Westminster Abbey
1682 Organist at the Chapel Royal, duties shared with Blow and Child
1683 Keeper of the royal instruments, on Hingston's death
1684 Member of the King's Private Music (chiefly as a keyboard player) after distinction at the coronation of James II
1684 Music for the coronation of William III. Contributions to Playford's *Harmonia Sacra*

The amount of music written for plays and musical spectacles suggests either that he had a retaining fee or that he received good payment from the theatres, as he did for the St Cecilia odes, and on such occasions as the Yorkshire Feast, a gathering of northern gentry in London, or the centenary celebrations of Trinity College, Dublin. He was surely paid also for the revision of Playford's 'Introduction to the Skill of Music'.

He was more prosperous than most musicians and, despite the enormous mass of composition he undertook, no evidence contradicts the impression that he was happy and easy-going. Portraits in fine clothes and with hair elaborately arranged (his own, not a wig) tell us less than we should like to know of his character. We have no reference to any illness before he was overtaken by an unspecified malady just before his death. It could have been pneumonia; or maybe he had the deceptively bright appearance and manner of the consumptive, for tuberculosis ran in the family and

[1] See *Purcell* by J. A. Westrup, in Dent's 'Master Musicians', or *Henry Purcell* by A. K. Holland, published by G. Bell & Sons.

three of his children died in infancy. His end came swiftly and he expected it, for he made his will on the day he died. His own music enriched his sumptuous funeral at the Abbey. Even allowing for the ornate and bombastic language of the times, the elegies composed by Blow and others sincerely express a loss that was deeply felt not only by members of Purcell's profession but by many more people than knew him personally.

Church and Religious Music

At the Restoration many people could not remember the English liturgy from Charles I's time. Liturgy is a fixed order of worship in which certain items vary, so as to be 'proper' to a day or season, but they also use prescribed texts. Not so are the words used in motets or anthems, chosen by musical directors for performance at a juncture in the rite. Tudor composers normally used the Psalms or other parts of Scripture, but devotional verse later entered church services in anthems before hymn books were in use. London gossips and diarists lead us to suppose that religion's witness to things unseen was not evident at the Chapel Royal. This we cannot assume, for the weekday offices were retained. When the King attended, however, we can be sure that the fashionable congregation enjoyed things both seen and heard. Among the latter were the choral responses, psalms and canticle settings, but the climactic attraction was the cantata-like anthem with instrumental symphonies, vocal solos, duets etc., and choruses.

The length of many a fine Restoration anthem justifies its absence from the cathedral repertory except at special music festivals. Liturgically the tail wagged the dog, probably to the delight of young Purcell who composed some forty anthems before he was twenty-five. We distinguish two types:

(i) *The Verse Anthem*, which treats the sentences sectionally. Those marked 'Verse', if not for solo voice, use only a single voice for each part. Those marked 'Full' engage the whole choir. Instrumental sections and passages, whether lengthy preludes or short ritornellos, are simply called symphonies.

(ii) *The Full Anthem*, which secures its main contrasts within a choral texture, though it may use short solo passages. Full anthems are often unaccompanied but Jacobean and Caroline composers copied organ parts, as Purcell did.

Though Purcell's anthems were for the Chapel Royal and Westminster Abbey we should not imagine each of the two types just mentioned to be allotted to one or the other foundation. Orchestral instruments were used at the Abbey only on special royal or national occasions, yet the shorter verse anthems were no doubt sung with organ; we also know that full anthems were used at the Chapel Royal although the King's attendance on Sundays must usually, if not always, have been marked by a sumptuous verse anthem, for he was not fond of the contrapuntal textures in full anthems which might obscure the words and deny the metrical rhythms which set the royal foot tapping.

Some of Purcell's early anthems are disappointingly undistinguished. His best work came during his last years, but his first attention to church music trained him to overcome tasks which face composers of any period. To *rely* on words and serve them 'twopence coloured' does not justify departure from spoken liturgy or drama. Verse anthems demanded purely musical invention during instrumental sections, a challenge to relate them to vocal sections, and a diversity of 'movements'. What are now called developments of themes, together with echoes, ritornellos, sequences and near-sequences, helped both forward movement and unification; but notable progress was made in recognising the value of tonality or key-distribution. Excursion from a key brought adventure; return to it clinched integration. Purcell's sequences may pass through a series of keys, whereas in older music 'modulation' meant cadencing on other notes than the tonic, rarely with a distinct shift of tonality. We may tire of cadences on C and G in an admirable Palestrina work. We are not aware of the limitation even in Purcell's popular 'Rejoice in the Lord alway', wherein the C major setting of that first verse recurs almost like a rondo refrain. (The suggestion of a peal in the opening symphony earned for this work the nickname of the 'Bell' anthem.)

It is not length alone nor lack of enterprise that keeps much of Purcell's church music out of liturgical repertory, however attractive it seems from broadcasts and recordings. The anthems that can be heard in cathedrals and churches with good choirs (for instance, 'Rejoice in the Lord alway', 'O God, thou hast cast us out', 'Thy word is a lantern') have not only instrumental sections that are effective when transcribed for organ, but also verse parts that do not demand some of Purcell's outstanding singers. Without 'that stupendous bass' at the Chapel Royal, the Rev. John Gostling, such passages as Ex. 7 withhold music from choirs that would like to use it. Moreover choirmasters favour music which fully engages all their singers. Despite Cooke's success with the boys, it took several years before they could be expected to tackle lengthy contributions to music for Sundays and weekdays, and congregations enjoyed hearing the fine soloists, adult and juvenile; it is therefore useful to analyse one of Purcell's most attractive verse anthems to illustrate both his response to these facts and the means by which sections were musically related.

Ex.7

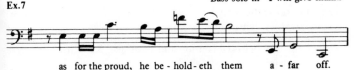

Bass solo in "I will give thanks"

as for the proud, he be - hold- eth them   a - far   off.

Of the 350 bars of 'My beloved spake' only 36 are 'full', 134 are taken by instrumental sections, and the rest by the single voices of 'verse' sections. One verse passage in this anthem is known to many parish choirs – that set to 'And the voice of the turtle is heard in our land'. Its memorable chord progressions were adapted to a psalm chant for Psalm 90, 'Lord thou hast been our refuge', used at funerals. In this analysis the number of bars is given against each section.

'My beloved spake', words from the Song of Solomon, *Ch. 2, vv. 10–16.*

1 (32) *Symphony.* Minuet tempo. Binary design with coda. The first violin part shows a melodic span not dependent on two-bar or four-bar units (Ex. 8 overleaf).

2 (15) *Verse.* A-T-B-B. 'My beloved spake . . . rise, my love, my fair one.'

   (5) *Symphony.* Coda-ritornello echoing vocal figuration.

   (19) *Verse.* Slower tempo and change to F minor. 'For lo, the winter is past.'

   (14) *Symphony.* Ritornello in F major. References to No. 1.

3 (27) *Verse.* A-T-B-B. 'The flowers on earth appear.' Return to brisk tempo for 'And the time of the singing of birds is come'.

   (13) *Full.* Repetition of 'And the time of the singing, etc.' Same music.

   (44) *Verse.* With string ritornellos and some references to No. 1. 'Hallelujah', followed by 'And the voice of the turtle is heard in our land' (Ex. 9 overleaf).

4 (32) *Symphony.* Exact repetition of No. 1.

5 (20) *Verse.* Tenor solo. 'The fig tree . . . and the vines.'

6 (9) *Verse.* A-T-B-B. 'Rise, my love, etc.'

(5) *Symphony*. Ritornello.
(28) *Verse*. 'My beloved is mine and I am his.'
(18) *Symphony*. Ritornello.
(23) *Verse*. 'Hallelujah!'
(10) *Symphony*. Ritornello.

7 (23) *Full*. 'My beloved is mine and I am his.' Repetition of verse music.

Ex.8   Opening symphony. "My beloved spake"

Ex.9

And the voice of the tur-tle is heard — in our

land, and the voice of the tur-tle is heard, ——

—— is heard in our land.

Though we cannot reproach modern choirmasters for making no liturgical use of such anthems, however attractive they are as music, it must be regretted that most of the half dozen early full anthems are not in use in all cathedrals, for none is of inordinate length. Many are most suitable for penitential seasons and solemn days; for example: 'Lord, how long wilt Thou be angry?', 'Hear my prayer, O Lord', 'Remember not, Lord, our offences', the first setting of 'Thou knowest, Lord, the secrets of all hearts' (not the one with trombones in the Queen Mary funeral music), and the second version of the funeral sentences 'In the midst of life we are in death'. To these can be added the superb S-S-A-T-B setting of the Latin psalm 'Jehovah, quam multi sunt hostes' which our better cathedral choirs do not neglect. The appearance of the direction 'verse' or 'first time verse; second time chorus' does not alter the conception of a full anthem; it merely gives a contrast within music of similar measure and speed and mood, as does the passing of a polyphonic sentence with a fugued point to a homophonic one. Moreover the organ part in these anthems is a support to the voices over the continuo bass, not a deliberately independent accompaniment. Some of Purcell's contemporaries must have regarded the full anthems as harking back to Tudor and Jacobean church music. In fact they are not archaic, but may be compared with the string fantasias which also contain masterly counterpoint and arresting harmony. If the chromatics of the eight-voice 'O Lord God of Hosts' had been only a feature in an archaic conception, Burney would neither have called the anthem 'extremely pathetic and expressive' nor declared that he experienced 'more pain than pleasure' from the daring harmony of the final measures, which delight our ears today.

After the mid-1680s Purcell wrote fewer anthems, and when he did, they were usually for special occasions. The most admired is the least adaptable to cathedral routine. 'My heart is inditing' was composed for the coronation of James II, for which the choirs of Westminster, Windsor and the Chapel Royal were combined. To those were added the royal instruments which alone could make most musicians classify the work as a verse anthem, yet its superb eight-part choral texture seems to crown that of all full anthems. Counterpoint is offset by massive homophony, and the choruses are developed in broader paragraphs than usual, so that short quotations would not show the essential magnificence. Lengthy extracts are quoted in Fellowes' *English Cathedral Music*, Westrup's *Purcell* in Dent's 'Master Musicians' series and Volume V of the *New Oxford History of Music*.

Of comparable magnificence is an honorific ode considered under 'Church Music' because it uses *Te Deum* and *Jubilate*. In 1694, the year before he died, Purcell set this tribute to his art for performance on St Cecilia's Day. Two years earlier he had composed one of his most ambitious odes, 'Hail, bright Cecilia!', for that festival – an artistic rather than a religious one. The ode had been set in the equivalent of separate arias and choruses, but Purcell's attempt to make the full and verse sections of *Te Deum* and *Jubilate* less distinctly separate makes us expect music which, however fine, is little more than one thing after another. Church musicians know *Te Deum* as a notoriously difficult text to integrate musically without using symphonic themes which, as they recur, are not always ideal for the passing words. Purcell was handicapped by limited key-change because of the two trumpets in D which are employed in exultant verses distributed throughout these canticles. Changes of key for short 'verse' passages soon lead back to the key of D, with which modern ears become surfeited, however much Purcell's listeners loved the splendour. (Similar trumpets contribute to the empty pomp of Handel's Dettingen *Te Deum* which, despite its oratorio-like spread, is inferior to his Utrecht setting composed thirty years earlier.) The Purcell work was so admired that it was given annually in St Paul's at festivals of the Sons of the Clergy until it was supplanted in 1713 by Handel's Utrecht *Te Deum*. To leave this last-period work of wonderful invention with nothing but the judgment we should apply to a modern setting would be grossly unfair. This can be seen if we imagine the first six verses of *Te Deum* offered as the same kind of full-yet-verse anthem as 'My heart is inditing', showing a similar command of variety and integration in a design calculated to prevent six laudatory verses from being one long and loud massive blaze. Well-judged climaxes of intensity govern the conception. Who else would begin the word-setting with a verse passage to bring the first climax at '*All* the earth doth worship thee'?

1 (12) *Symphony*.

2 (10) *Verse*. 'We praise thee, O God: we acknowledge thee to be the Lord', using the trumpet motive (French style) from the symphony.

3 (20) *Full.* Entry from bass to high soprano repeating the word 'all' until, at maximum sonority of instruments and voices, in a well-spaced D major chord, comes '*All* the earth doth worship thee'. Fugued entries lead 'the Father everlasting'.

4 (30) *Verse.* (S-S-B) and *Full*, Beginning in A minor with imitative entries 'To thee all angels cry aloud' the Verse moves back to D major. The two sopranos continue 'To thee cherubin and seraphin continually, continually, continually do cry' with three separated detonations of 'Holy!' by choir, strings, organ and trumpets, the last 'Holy' proceeding to 'Lord God of Sabaoth'. The final massive climactic passage uses all forces in homophony — 'Heaven and earth are full of thy glory'.

Today we may be glad that in church music Purcell did not set long portions of his texts in recitative-like declamation. (Italian audiences had many years before grumbled about *Il tedio del recitativo* in dramatic music.) Nor, though music in general was moving towards the Italianate high baroque style which we know best from Handel, did Purcell often depart as far from English idiom and so nearly anticipate the Handel styles as he does in the 1688 anthem 'O sing unto the Lord'. Purely English and distinctively his own are the simple trombone chords for the march, along with the anthems, including the newly-composed 'Thou knowest Lord the secrets of all hearts', heard at Queen Mary's funeral, to be used six months later at his own. Surely there is no need to quote from these marvels, but we may do so from Tudway's comments: 'I appeal to all who were present . . . whether they ever heard anything so rapturously fine and solemn . . . which drew tears from all, and yet a plain, natural composition.'

Today the 'service' (or setting of the canticles) heard in one of our choral foundations may be set more ambitiously than the anthem. Evidently this never happened in the Restoration Chapel Royal, for the few settings of either morning or evening canticles which we inherit from its composers suggest that, with the cathedrals, the Chapel Royal used a repertory of older and chiefly 'full' settings which treated the canticles more efficiently than colourfully, and avoided repetition of words. Such were and still are the best-known settings by Tallis, Byrd, Morley and Gibbons. Neither does Purcell's G minor Evening Service 'spread' or repeat words except in the two treatments of *Gloria Patri*, and the first of those, to *Magnificat*, makes only a single repetition of 'is now' and 'and ever'; the second, to *Nunc dimittis*, is much more elaborate. The first verse is set to a canon '4-in-2 at the octave' of masterly craftsmanship; the composer then changes from verse to full and resumes 'French style' at 'as it was in the beginning' with a rest after 'in' which sounds and surely *is* offensive, and the offence is repeated after the bass solo 'is now and ever shall be'. There follows a lengthy verse texture to the much repeated 'Amen', the vocal counterpoint sounding over a bass *ostinato* of descending semitones, its final presentation underlying five 'Amens' sung full. Apart from this questionable, if musically climactic and interesting last *Gloria*, this bright little service seems one of the most attractive, and it is hard to understand why Fellowes and others feel cool towards it.[1] (Fellowes thinks it has too many 'verse' passages, but in liturgical context these provide the antiphony of *cantoris* and *decani* in concertato with the full sections.)

The B flat service comprises not merely *Te Deum*, *Benedictus*, *Magnificat* and *Nunc dimittis*, but all the alternative canticles (for example *Benedicite* and *Cantate Domino*) for the morning and evening offices as well as the *Kyrie* and *Credo* for the Communion Service. Choir settings of further eucharistic texts were not customary, despite their use in the 'High Service' as it is called in Laudian part-books.[2] Purcell's B-flat settings are largely dignified and homophonic, recalling older church music except when harmonic boldness betrays their authorship. The *Benedicite* (alternative morning canticle to the *Te Deum*) is particularly brilliant, and in places throughout the service, notably settings of *Gloria Patri*, occur canons 4-in-2, 3-in-1, and so on, that are not merely ingenious but as musical as their contexts of solid and more plain texture. 'Far more impressive than many a more pretentious work' is Westrup's verdict; yet this is not the music to choose for concert listening, whereas the spritely G minor Evening Service has an immediate appeal to listeners who are not well acquainted with Anglican choir music.

The 'and religious music' in our title implies that a few pieces not originally composed for the church have proved admirably suitable

[1] E. H. Fellowes (1870–1951), *English Cathedral Music*, London 1941.

[2] 'High Service' is a translation from *Hauptgottesdienst*. English high churchmen envied the Lutherans whose main Sunday worship was eucharistic (as well as musically and ceremonially elaborate) until the Pietist changes which Bach opposed. Children, including choristers, left after the Nicene Creed, the rest of the service being for Communicants. A similar practice is still remembered in some English cathedrals.

for certain services. The first piece in Playford's *Harmonia Sacra* (1688) is 'Now that the sun hath veil'd his light', the beautiful 'Hymn on a Ground Bass' which, though imagined for domestic solo singing with harpsichord continuo (the bass perhaps best lightly reinforced by gamba or cello), sounds lovely from boys' voices with organ when used as an evening anthem. Less suitable for the purpose are the declamatory items in the collection: for instance, the settings of Jeremy Taylor's 'Great God and just' and George Herbert's 'With sick and famish'd eyes', despite their outstanding attention to the accent and meaning of the words. Some of these sacred songs are like Italian solo cantatas, with recitative, arioso and aria sections. Recently 'The Blessed Virgin's Expostulation' has become deservedly popular with recitalists. It deals with Mary's anxiety when the boy Jesus was 'sought sorrowing' until found 'sitting among the doctors' in the Temple. Inconceivable except for female solo voice, it is too subjective for liturgy even when the event to which it refers is commemorated. A similar comment can apply to the unique 'In guilty night', a dramatic scena for three voices (S-A-B) and continuo, which deals with King Saul's consultation of the Witch of Endor.

Several Purcell works issued as 'hymns' or 'psalms' are what we should call part-songs to religious texts and would make useful short anthems, especially on 'Men only' days. Examples are 'Lord, not to us' (A-T-B) and 'Since God so tender a regard' (T-T-B). The English Reformation, unlike the German, did not bring other hymns than metrical psalms into congregational use. The Methodist movement created a new demand, and Charles Wesley's 'Love divine, all loves excelling' was originally sung to Purcell's 'Fairest Isle' melody. Purcell's name, however, does occur twice in standard hymn books. The tune 'Burford' is taken from Chetham's *Psalmody* (1718), and 'Belville' from *The Psalmist* (1842). The latter, compiled from the Hallelujahs at the end of an anthem, is also known as 'Westminster Abbey', having been revived by Sir Sydney Nicholson when Organist of the Abbey in the years 1918 to 1928.

As the seventeenth century approached the eighteenth, the most attractive chamber music for royal and privileged ears was the newest – that purveyed by orchestras, not consorts of single instruments such as viols, recorders, trombones and so on. Several violins or violas playing a part in unison make a different sound from that of one instrument amplified; they also have a far bigger range of tone, from a loud staccato or pizzicato accent to a soft, silky or nebulous evocation of sentiment.[1] Italian citizens enjoyed the orchestral sound as church music, as in the university basilica of S. Petronio, Bologna, famous for *sinfonie* with trumpets and strings; in Venice they enjoyed it as theatre music; but Londoners were the first to hear it in public concerts. Whereas Philidor's *concert spirituel* in Paris was not promoted until 1725, Charles II's orchestral director, John Banister, began his public concerts in 1672. They were continued by Britton, who attracted Pepusch and Handel to his charcoal loft in Clerkenwell. Yet Banister advertised chiefly solo virtuosi, and his ensembles may have engaged as few instruments as delighted us in theatres and cinemas before we had domestic radio. Possibly larger orchestras were heard at taverns which had built large new music rooms. That at the Mitre in Wapping reminded the *London Spy* of a church with its organ 'in a fine gallery' and the players in an area 'like a railed chancel', while at the Globe in Greenwich Pepys saw a 'woman with a rod in her hand keeping time to the musique'.[2]

What orchestral music was played either before the court or at these concerts is not fully known. Purcell became Composer in Ordinary for the Violins when he was eighteen, yet the catalogue of his works in *Grove* includes only three pieces which we may hear at an orchestral concert, and we have no evidence that the composer

---

[1] A *Zufallsorchester*, such as the large and heterogeneous assemblage for Monteverdi's early operas, is not an orchestra as we know it. The true orchestral sound came into public Italian opera when theatre directors standardised casts and numbers of players. The latter formed a basic complement of strings, all of the violin, not the viol type, which could support the harmony without continuo if necessary. Even if smaller than most modern string orchestras it was adequate when combined with trumpets, oboes, or whatever wind instruments a composer demanded.

[2] Ned Ward: *The Complete Modern London Spy* or *A real, new and universal disclosure of the secret nocturnal and diurnal transactions in and about London written by a gentleman of fortune,* 18 parts (1698–9), 2 vols.

envisaged such treatment; they are the Chacony, and the Pavan, both in G minor 'in four parts', listed under 'Music for strings without continuo', and the Sonata in D major, listed under 'Music for trumpet, strings and continuo'.[1] We may understand the puzzle if we turn to the corresponding list of Lully's works, which mentions *none* for orchestra by that first famous conductor! We know that suites (consisting of a French overture and shorter pieces in dance rhythms) supplied the first orchestral repertory purveyed not only to Louis XIV but to princelings from Rhineland to the Danube. Their orchestras were enlarged to perform music by Lully, Campra, Destouches and others until their own musicians composed better suites. These were soon ousted by the second repertory – Italian concertos – which in its turn was to be ousted by a third, Mannheim-style symphonies. (Bach's suites or 'Ouvertures' were among the last of their kind, but many of Handel's concertos are shaped like suites.)

The fact is that, as Lully's orchestral chamber music came from his many ballets and operas, so Purcell's came from overtures, 'symphonies' and 'airs' in his dramatic works and odes, and from incidental music for plays. Though it inherited no repertory, the comparatively new orchestral sound in London was loved. Ben Jonson complained that it was more enthusiastically received than the spoken parts of plays. His contemporary, Theophilus Cibber, wrote of a man who 'came to hear the First and Second Music . . . but prudently retired, taking his money again at the doors before the Third Music', for he could claim it if he did not stop for the play. Concert performances of Purcell's theatre music are therefore justified, and one could wish they were more frequent. Some of the best short pieces come from his last years, as do contributions to *The Gordian Knot Untied* and *Sir Anthony Love* (1691), *The Old Bachelor* (1693), *Bonduca* and *Abdelazer* (1695). The greatest extended orchestral pieces are the longer 'symphonies' and overtures, and it seems strange that modern conductors, willing to include baroque works which do not employ the full orchestra as understood by Beethoven, begin their concerts with a limited choice of overtures which have been recorded over and over again, when they could use such thrilling pieces as the overture to the 1692 St Cecilia Ode (continuous but with six changes of tempo), or that to the 1694

[1] *Grove's Dictionary of Music and Musicians*, 5th edn (1954), ed. Eric Blom.

Ode for the birthday of Queen Mary, 'Come ye sons of art'. Outstanding in its magnificence is the 'Trumpet Overture' introducing the masque in *The Indian Queen* – not the first overture, although that finishes with a trumpet flourish. Rather lengthy quotations are made at Ex. 10 from a work which one would expect to be as well known to English listeners as any piece from Handel's *Water Music* or *Fireworks Music*.

Ex.10   Trumpet Overture (Most middle parts omitted)

(a) *Opening*

[14 bars]

(b) *Canzona*   [**Allegro**]

Strings. Trumpet joins later.

[48 bars]

(c) *Final section*

Tr.

tr

Slow

Strings
only

tr

There are no pocket scores of these overtures, nor can some of
the finest be judged by piano reductions in vocal scores. What may
therefore seem inordinate space is taken to show just the beginning
and ending of the example from *The Indian Queen* so that we may
notice a continuity or spread of musical thought which distinguishes
Purcell from Lully – indeed distinguishes him from most composers

27

before Berlioz. True, that first swagger for the natural trumpet takes only two bars and has few melodic equals, but how the harmony and contrapuntal imitations (asterisked) carry the texture forward! After the pompous introduction, what Purcell calls the canzona, because of its free fugato, is made of small enough units to enable him to modulate and yet include short contributions from the trumpet; but at its conclusion we again marvel at a slow nine bars which press forward without reliance on metrical accents. The expansiveness of the work is as admirable as its brilliance.

The only other long pieces usable in orchestral concerts are the chaconnes. Though in the same manuscript as the Fantazias (with one instrument to each part) the G minor Chacony and Pavan are heard from string orchestras with the added part for double-bass. Another fine G minor chaconne adds a viola part to the unusual Sonata No. 6 of Purcell's second set. There are valid reasons for rarely making concert use of chaconnes already orchestral in Purcell's dramatic works, for instance 'The Grand Dance' in *King Arthur*, or 'The Triumphing Dance' in *Dido and Aeneas*. They are impressive with the stage setting, and would be less so if they were not musically simple for the dignified, courtly dances. The unique interest of a piece like the G minor Chacony, intended for *listening* to (i.e. as chamber music), lies in the arrival of upper melodies in phrases which do not correspond in length with the bass. They therefore overlap the junctures at which the ground finishes and begins afresh, often preventing a full close at that point. The bass theme may itself be varied or shortened or lengthened to cause welcome key changes.

Lully, whose effect on the course of music in his own country and outside it is incalculable, is not disparaged by a tribute to those Purcell treatments of a ground bass that were unlike his. Lully's chaconnes came where he needed pomp, with variations of texture rather than melody over a four-bar or eight-bar bass that the dancers could follow in its regular lengths, each with a distinct close. The metrical rhythm was so prominent that we almost hear the tap of the mace-baton as it hits the floor on the first beat of each triple measure. (A wound which festered after the baton had pierced his foot brought about Lully's death.) Though the design is loose, such chaconnes need not be formless. Their inexorable progress may incur a thinning of texture or a variation or two in the minor key before an increase of power during a final section. Often trumpets join as the whole cast comes to its last spectacular formation, perhaps with the king on stage to complete the tableau. Even when emulating Lully for a similar stage finale, Purcell did not always resist the exercise of musical adventure. We see at Ex. 11a the formal opening of 'The Triumphing Dance', but at Ex. 11b the bass figure is transferred to the uppermost part, and a fugal entry leads to such variation of the bass itself as will bring about a modulation to G major.

Ex.11

(a)   Dido and Aeneas. "The Triumphing Dance"

Inner parts omitted.

(b)

In his revision of *An Introduction to the Skill of Music* Purcell declared composition upon a ground to be 'easy', as it is at the level just described: but in the same treatise we read: 'Good Air ought to be preferred before Nice Rules', which means 'Vital melody can flaunt harmonic convention'. Using the word 'tautology' he attacks stagnant basses. The clashes that spice Purcell's textures and delight modern ears come from independent lines or strands that were not devised merely to suit the continuo bass or chord sequence. Lully could produce melodies admirably suited to French prosody, but the middle parts of his instrumental music lack the linear interest of Purcell's, which are most attractive in ground-bass treatments that are not danced chaconnes. Some of these works prepare for contrapuntal interest by avoiding a square four-bar or eight-bar bass. The grounds of Dido's 'When I am laid in earth' and the Evening Hymn, 'Now that the sun hath veil'd his light', are five bars long; that of the song in *Oedipus*, 'Music for a while shall all your cares beguile', is three bars long. Contrivance to ensure phrase-overlapping and modulation is beautifully hidden in the ground-bass items of some of the St Cecilia Odes, for instance 'See the glittering Ruler of the Day' (1690) and 'Here the deities approve' (1683). The latter was published in *Orpheus Britannicus* (a collection of Purcell's music for solo voice) and is also arranged for harpsichord and called 'A New Ground' in *Musick's Handmaid, Part 2*, 1689. Like Purcell, we could profitably perform with instruments alone some of the pieces on ground-basses that at present include voices. A sample from 'Here the deities approve' is shown at Ex. 12 because adequate sections from the G minor Chacony would be difficult to keep short or to display on two staves.

If the foregoing comments were drastically condensed they would be replaced by: 'Purcell not only practised counterpoint assiduously, self-disciplined and/or guided by Blow, but loved it despite what was admired by influential instructors during his boyhood.' We recognise the fact in textures that parade no contrapuntal devices. The string fantasias, most of which date from as early as 1680, give the most direct testimony to his own taste, and to his determination to serve his art and not merely the taste of court and society. Like Bach's 'Forty-Eight', these works circulated in manuscript for the delight of truly musical persons in their homes.[1]

---

[1] They were first printed by Curwen in the Warlock-Mangeot edition of 1927. Philip Heseltine (1894–1930), who composed under the name of Peter Warlock while acting as a music columnist and editor under his own, allowed an impecunious student to copy his sheets before he sent them to

Ex.12

Ode (St. Cecilia). "Welcome to all the pleasures"

They might have been played on viols or 'modern' instruments. We know that some music lovers possessed both, and may even have mixed them. (Arguments favouring one or the other can be read elsewhere.) Certainly many devotees of the English 'fancy' or fantasia must have kept their viols, for this kind of chamber music had been uniquely pursued in England from Tudor times and through the Commonwealth period, Purcell's tributes forming a last and crowning glory of the genre.

Players had collections of parts by Byrd, Morley, Dering, the Gibbons and the Lawes brothers, Ferrabosco, Wilson, Lupo and

press. One effect was to make him read textbooks of so-called counterpoint only for amusement; another was a determination to teach counterpoint (as R. O. Morris did) only from such great examples as Purcell and Bach.

many others; Purcell is likely to have taken special interest in chamber music by Locke – to his profit; for Locke saw no sense in forcing exact imitation, or any other procedure demanded only by Beckmessers, to the detriment of musical progress and appeal. Just as Bach felt free to vary a fugue subject, to make entries at varying distances, to use or avoid regular countersubjects and so on, so Locke put shape and rhythm before 'nice rules'. We see at Ex. 13 the differing intervals at different entries of the 'point' or fugue-subject of a four-part fantasia. Morley describes what he calls a 'Fancy' as allowing the composer to take 'a point at his pleasure' – devise and treat it as he wishes. The number of movements is not prescribed, and therefore neither is the number of points; the fancy or fantasia in many ways resembled the former church motet which, however, moved to a new point for a new sentence or phrase while the development of a previous one was still finishing; but the fugued movements of a consort fantasia were usually short and dealt with only one point each. Otherwise, before the later development of fugue design, with episodes and key-schemes like Bach's, mere entries, even with *stretti*, would pall.

Ex.13

Locke

Purcell normally uses three (sometimes four) movements, that is sections of different speeds, the middle or slow ones tending to be very short. The openings of the three movements of the eighth four-part fantasia are shown at Ex. 14. The first has no speed indication but seems to suggest *andante con moto*. It lasts for twenty-five bars, connective material not advancing any second point. The second movement, 'Drag', takes only seven bars; it does not use a point so much as the three-crotchet anacrusic rhythm as a means of binding the arresting harmony. The third movement, 'Brisk', does propose a point, very freely treated as it comes to climax in twenty bars. The fifteen fantasias are as follows: three of three parts; nine of four parts; one of five parts ('Fantasia upon one note' – the lower or

Ex.14

Four-part Fantasia No. 8

(i)

(ii) **"Drag"**

(iii) **"Brisk"**

tenor viol (or viola) maintaining 'middle C' through all three movements); one of six parts and one of seven parts, both 'In Nomine'.
'In Nomine' is short for 'In Nomine Domini', and refers to the anti-
phon *Gloria tibi Trinitas* – a plainchant which held an inexplicable
fascination for English composers from the mid-sixteenth century
until Purcell. The notes were laid out as a *cantus firmus*, in plain
breves or other equal lengths, usually in the tenor, the other parts
pursuing contrapuntal points. Possibly the surmounting of the task
by Taverner, Blitheman, Bull and others excited the emulation of
others, so that 'A Nominy' became a proof of professional ability.
Even Purcell's ingenuity seems to some ears unable to make quite
as fine music under this restriction as it does when free to deal with
a point of his own devising. It is therefore all the more wonderful
that the greater limitation imposed by the 'Fantasia upon one note'
brings something far more enjoyable than a display of contrapuntal
facility.

Even so, the most interesting music, the most beautiful 'lines',
come in the three-part and four-part fantasias where, so to speak,
there is more room for adventure. Earlier in this guide Ex. 4b
(page 10) showed the taut imitation in the first section of the fourth
four-part fantasia – one of the shortest and most beautiful in the set.
One cannot resist quoting its closing bars at Ex. 15.

To be fine music, counterpoint cannot be pursued as an isolated
technique. It was once a synonym for harmony; that is, any vital
movement in parts. It invigorates music not just by disagreement

Ex.15   End of Four-part Fantasia No. 4

or recalcitrance of rhythms, but by a parallel play of discord and concord as understood at this or that period of musical history. We do not tell the whole truth by saying that these fantasias pay tribute to an outmoded practice such as Purcell observed in 'full' anthems and service settings; they are of their day and composer. Nor do we flatter Purcell by saying that, at twenty-one, he was 'almost' as accomplished a contrapuntist as young Bach; still less by the silly observation that he 'points to Bach'. Bach achieved a balance between harmonic progression (by his time consolidated and conventionalised by the continuo practice) and 'horizontal thinking'. For all his daring it was more restricted than Purcell's which, had he known it, might have fascinated him but seemed rough. Yet in his later chamber works, the sonatas, Purcell himself showed (and declared) submission to the smoothness furthered by the continuo practice.

So he may have believed and certainly wished others to believe, yet we do well to let music speak for itself before lending credence to composers' remarks upon their works. (Those who believe that *Tristan* makes music the servant and not the master of the drama will believe any composer.) We therefore use a little salt as we peruse the preface to *Twelve Sonatas of Three Parts*, 1683. Frances Purcell, the composer's widow, collected a further *Ten Sonatas in Four Parts*, composed at various times but published in 1697 with a preface that tells us they 'had already found many friends'. Henry Playford (1657–1706) may have drafted both prefaces!

1. *Three or Four Parts*? The 'four' designates no different outlay from the earlier 'three'. There were no printed scores. For both sets buyers could obtain four parts at Purcell's house or at Playford and Carr's premises. They were for two violins, a 'bass' (gamba or cello) and a second bass which was figured for organ or harpsichord continuo. It differs in several places from the other 'bass' (the two are combined on the lowermost stave of Ex. 16) and Purcell's preface declares that he did not originally intend to issue the continuo bass. Figures or not, anyone who plays continuo in Purcell without careful preparation and fails to come to grief may consider *se valde profecisse* in the art.

2. *'Seriousness and gravity'*. Italian masters were emulated, we are informed, principally 'to bring the seriousness and gravity of that sort of Musick into vogue and reputation among our Country-men' who 'should begin to loath the levity and balladry of our neighbours' (the French?). As Mrs Squeers would say: 'There's richness for you!' – from him who left us convivial settings of balladry and lubricious rounds and catches for tavern company.

3. *'I have faithfully endeavoured a just imitation'* (of 'the most famed Italian masters'). Though chiefly good advertisement, this needs consideration. The Italian whom Purcell calls 'famous' in Playford's *Introduction* is one Lelio Calista of whom we know only what the late W. Barclay Squire told us – that some thirty manuscripts of his trio sonatas are in English libraries but none has been found elsewhere. He called his main fugued movements 'canzonas' as Purcell did in overtures as well as sonatas. Other scholars believe that Purcell was acquainted with sonatas by G. B. Vitali who died in 1692, but speculation about the supposed models is quite unimportant, for Purcell's endeavour to imitate was certainly not strenuous.

The only evidence that matters is from the music, not a preface that a later age would rightly have entitled 'Advertisement'. The style by which we should judge a change from English waywardness would have clear harmony moving towards undisguised cadential formulae finishing balanced, symmetrical phrases, and as conven-

Ex.16   Sonata 4, second set

tional a key-scheme as that of the *da capo* aria already dominating
Italian opera while Purcell lived. Most readers know the style from
Handel, Telemann and younger composers than Purcell, but the
extraordinary popularity of Corelli's sonatas did much to commend
the high baroque features just mentioned. Corelli's first book of
sonatas was printed so closely before Purcell's that it may not have
been sampled before Purcell composed them; but what prevented
his knowing sonatas by Legrenzi, Stradella, Cazzati, the Vitalis
(father and son), Ruggieri, Torelli, the elder Bononcini, Taglietti,
Veracini . . . ? 'What! will the line stretch out to the crack of doom?'
one asks with Macbeth. The British Museum alone can tell us that
such music was here in quantities, brought over by travellers as
well as musicians. Purcell worked with Matteis, Draghi and other
Italians whose violin technique astonished London, and with fine
players like Mell and Baltzar. It is ridiculous to imagine that a man
of Purcell's ability could not, *if he wished*, have produced something
far nearer Corelli than he did, though we may be thankful that he
did not. The beauty of Corelli is enchanting for one sample sonata,
but somewhat enervating if one plays straight through a set,
whereas to play a series of Purcell sonatas is a bracing experience.

To support this belief we quote at Ex. 17 something to compare with Ex. 16. It is from a trio sonata by another violinist in Charles II's band, William Young, who migrated to Innsbruck during the Commonwealth. That explains Italian influence but also brings to notice another Englishman from whom Purcell *must* have known a more 'just imitation' of Italian models than he himself intended to undertake. (To save space Exx. 17 and 18 give only a first violin part with a bass transposed up an octave to go on the treble stave.) Young published eleven sonatas (some specifically for violins) in 1653 – thirty years before Purcell's first set – and dedicated them to the Archduke of Austria to whom he was chamber musician; but he wrote more than these, and Ex. 17 is taken from one of those in Durham Cathedral Library, edited by Prof. Peter Evans (Schott, 1956). Obviously Purcell could have been as suave as Young, but as the fantasias tell us, he had a mind of his own and is loved because he managed to please the fashionable music-lovers without pandering to them. Applied to music, 'intellectual' is a metaphor, as also is even 'musical thought'. Yet how else can we describe what we admire in a composer to whom these metaphors can be applied,

Ex.17   William Young

despite the ravishing beauty of his simplest melodies? Naturally the style of the fantasias did not suit continuo harmony, nor even the clear discourse of two violins. How different, however, would the sonatas be if they were not by the composer of the fantasias!

None of the foregoing comments dismisses Purcell's preface as no more than advertising humbug. Movement towards Italian ideals (deplored by Holst and Whittaker) was a fact, and we are not wise after the Preface when we sense in many of the sonatas, even more in such near-Italian arias as 'Prepare thy conquest, love' (*Dido and Aeneas*) or 'Hark, the echoing air' (*The Fairy Queen*), Purcell's cautious swimming in the general current. Despite the exchange of contrapuntal themes – sometimes sheer contrapuntal virtuosity – between the parts, despite the English galliard rhythm in many movements, despite the harmonic false relations, the sonatas of the second set are even more Italianate than those of the first set. It is significant that they all favour the 'church' rather than the 'chamber' pattern, and the interplay of counterpoint excels Corelli's even when a bright fugue subject strikes us as very Italian.[1] Chromatic basses are also very English – or very Purcellian – and the slow movements are romantically emotional, particularly the one in no. 9 of the second set, which seems to be overplayed at the expense of others because at some time it got nicknamed the 'Golden Sonata'. To illustrate an undeniable movement towards Italian style (hardly a 'just imitation'!) we choose a violin-and-transposed-bass from a sonata in neither of the two sets (Ex. 18 overleaf). Evidently it was left unfinished, and so became called the 'Violin sonata in G minor'. The late Thurston Dart convincingly proved, however, that the continuo bass failed to supply the fugal and thematic imitations which were obviously intended to be played by a second string instrument, and his reconstruction is utterly convincing. It is a fine work.[2]

[1] The normal *da chiesa* pattern in the seventeenth century was: short slow introduction followed by the main first movement; a 'middle' *largo* and a brisk finale. The *sonata da camera* might begin with a fast movement like an *allemande*, followed by an indefinite number of movements in dance rhythms; it was in fact like a suite. Yet even Corelli sometimes forgot not to write such a title as 'Gavotta' in the course of a church sonata, and plenty of church sonatas were played in music rooms as chamber music. On the whole the church sonata, with or without slow introduction, is the ancestor of the classical sonata.

[2] Novello, 1959.

Ex.18

(a) *Middle movt.*

Purcell: Sonata in G minor

(b) *Finale*

Purcell's keyboard works are, on the whole, disappointing by comparison with German and French suites of the period, and one cannot endorse Westrup's opinion that the best of them, in the suites issued by Mrs Purcell and dedicated to the princess who was to become Queen Anne, 'are worthy predecessors of Bach's'. The most enjoyable of the harpsichord pieces are the little dances and airs, many arranged from theatre music. Westrup admits that the organ pieces 'do not represent Purcell at his best . . . if indeed they are his'. It is hard to believe that the organist of the Chapel Royal and Westminster Abbey improvised nothing better than that feeble voluntary on the 'Old Hundredth'.

Purcell's titles 'Ode' and 'Welcome Song' denote similar works which today would be called cantatas. A welcome song was elicited by the return of the monarch from Windsor or Winchester, or of a prince from abroad or the battlefield. The number of such works, some flagrantly sycophantic, others affectionately honorific (for example, those for birthdays of the beloved Queen Mary), suggest overwork on the part of a composer whose last dozen years produced a wealth of theatre and dramatic music; but Purcell enjoyed what many a composer has longed for – the certainty of hearing his music well performed. This may explain the fact that his output of odes exceeded the number that his appointment demanded. The Purcell Society volumes contain five welcome songs for Charles II and three for James II, six odes for the birthdays of Queen Mary and four for St Cecilia's Day, an ode for the marriage of Prince George of Denmark to Princess Anne, one for the Duke of Gloucester's birthday, one for the Yorkshire Feast, one for Louis Maidwell's school (to words by a pupil), and one for the centenary of Trinity College, Dublin. The list is not complete; other works of this kind have not been retrieved.

In view of future commentary here it should be mentioned that in many a year and for many an occasion – even the Dublin celebrations – Blow as well as Purcell composed an ode. Purcell's have considerable documentary as well as aesthetic value. They show his general advance during years of established eminence, and his particular advance in dealing with texts that offered no dramatic thread or series of scenes. We are not often likely to hear the earliest welcome songs, those of 1680–4. We should hear one or two of their solos and duets if the words made sense in isolated performance. On the whole, however, and especially in certain almost perfunctory choruses, we expect better; but we are unfair if we think the composer of those superb string fantasias was satisfied. (I am not suggesting that he supplied poor or even hasty music.) Purcell had absorbed from a long succession of composers the art whereby the fantasias made inconceivable any later and greater examples of the genre. Like the quartets of classical symphonists they are for the intimate relish of connoisseurs, being for similar instruments which, even when in unison instead of dialogue, give an effect of being loud although the actual decibel output is not high. The ode was not for lovers of intimate polyphony. It needed the direct impact of brilliance and pomp with sections to offset the sound of full voices or instruments; but the words supplied might not easily suggest certain contrasts provided in a play or drama, for example some expressing tenderness or pathos. In short, Purcell's appointment brought him to a genre which he had not learnt from anyone else.

Oh? Not Blow? No; surprisingly enough, Purcell had written three welcome odes for Charles II before Blow, in 1682, supplied 'Great Sir, the joy of all our hearts'. Both composers produced their first really fine odes for St Cecilia celebrations, but Purcell's led in 1683 with 'Welcome to all the pleasures', which we often enjoy by radio, whereas Blow's first St Cecilia Ode is 'Begin the Song' for 1684.[1] The two works have much in common – a 'French' overture for the strings, an invitatory and welcoming solo before the first chorus, independent symphonies and 'framing' ritornelli, a solo (in Blow a duet) on a ground-bass and an impressive final chorus. Solos and single-voice items are marked 'verse'. Surely the first model for the ode was the verse anthem. As the St Cecilia festivals grew grander, so did the orchestra – recorders, oboes, trumpets, drums – and the scale of the odes. Some sections approached a Handelian style, and Handel is said to have found in them the kind of choral settings London liked. The score of the most famous of Purcell's St Cecilia odes, that of 1692, occupies more than four times as many pages as the score of the 1683 one, which is not only worth frequent performance but interesting for its advances in design, with a remarkable key-scheme and a complex of final sections which justifies their grouping as a finale.

[1] It is thought that the St Cecilia Festivals began in London (then Oxford and Edinburgh) in 1683, when 'The Musical Society' attended service in St Bride's, Fleet Street, with fine music and a sermon defending music in worship – no doubt very anti-puritan. The gathering then went to Stationers' Hall for the Ode, followed by a dinner. The festivals were not always in the same places, for they became more sumptuous and public, at least musically. In 1683 Purcell wrote another Cecilian tribute, *Laudate Ceciliam*, which may have been the anthem in the church. The magnificent *Te Deum* and *Jubilate* of 1694 was not a necessary choice just because 22 November came on a Sunday, for in the following year Blow set the same canticles for the festival. Indeed the older man seems to have learnt from the younger.

'Welcome to all the pleasures', 1683.

E minor

1 *Overture* (strings). Slow, 16 bars of 4/4; fast (canzona), 40 bars of 3/4.
2 *Verse.* ATB. 'Welcome etc.'. Responding chorus: 'Hail, great assembly of Apollo'.
3 *Symphony.* Binary form.
4 Counter-tenor solo. 'Here the deities approve'. (Quoted at Ex. 12. Later arranged as *A New Ground* for harpsichord.) The strings continue the ground for 28 bars, then lead into the finale.

Finale:
C major

1 Verse SST. 'With joys celestial'. French style; 26 bars of 3/4.
2 Symphony. Binary in the style of the previous verse. Without repeats 24 bars.
3 Bass solo. 'Then lift up your voices', taken up by chorus; verse ATB continues with new words, but the chorus repeats 'Then lift up your voices' with an instrumental coda going to E minor.

E minor

4 Tenor solo: 'Beauty, thou scene of love'. Binary ritornello finishing in E major.

E major

5 The tenor solo is resumed with 'In a consort of voices' (16 bars) which is taken up by a full and loud chorus, beginning fugato. Towards the end there is a diminuendo to 'Iô Cecilia!', so that at last we hear only tenors, then basses, almost whispering 'Cecilia, Cecilia!' – a unique stroke of imagination.

The integration achieved in this 'finale' may be imagined by reading the text it covers and wondering how it could be disposed among the performers to maintain unity, continuity, variety and the right points of expectation and climax. The first couplet defies grammatical structure. Presumably 'their' refers to 'deities' in the counter-tenor solo, separated from this 'finale' by twenty-eight bars for strings only! The words of this doggerel were by one Fishburn. Purcell was often served with worse.

> While joys celestial their bright souls invade
> To find what great improvements you have made,
> Then lift up your voices, those organs of nature,
> Those charms to the troubled and amorous creature.
> The pow'r shall divert us a pleasanter way,
> For sorrow and grief find from music relief,
> And love its soft charms must obey.
> Beauty, thou scene of love, and Virtue, thou innocent fire,
> Made by the pow'rs above to temper the heat of desire;
> Music that fancy employs in rapture of innocent flame

We offer with lute and with voice to Cecilia's bright name
In a consort of voices, while instruments play,
With music we celebrate this holy day.
    Iô Cecilia!

If a text provides imagery, not just philosophising or moral sentiment, it suggests moods or veins of expression, so that a composer of genius can make even a stilted poetaster's verse *seem* to flower into poetry. The repeated phrases of a chorus or the single words on which a soloist lingers may disarm criticism of the text as a whole. During performances of the odes one recalls no outright laughter such as greets Nahum Tate's 'And let forsaken Dido die' at a point in the opera where it is least welcome. (Advice to producers: boldly change it to something like 'And let me here forsaken die'.)

To illustrate this point, it is worth digressing to comment upon a single song because most readers are likely to know it. The words of 'Music for a while shall all your cares beguile, wond'ring how your pains were eas'd, etc., are from *Oedipus*, in which Dryden collaborated. The sad but lovely setting (in a minor key) seems to respond to the idea of music soothing cares and pains. To that any passing image is incidental and does not halt the flow to accommodate striking onomatopoeia at 'till the snakes drop, drop, drop, drop, drop . . . from her head', the rests between each 'drop' (as Purcell's use of rests elsewhere) being unusually effective. With one prolonged emotion this song can hold a listener who knows nothing of Alecto and her snakes; the words might as well be 'shall all your cares beguile, though the tears drop, drop . . . from your eyes'. The point is made to negate the belief that Purcell is impressive in his later years either because texts more suited to music were forthcoming or because he became more sensitive to words. As perusal of that 1683 text has shown, words served *musical* designs; they did not determine them. Sometimes verbal imagery set the musical puppets dallying, but often only incidentally, as did Alecto's snakes; this applies even when Purcell had Schubert's freedom to choose among lyric verses for his separate songs. True, no musician set English more admirably, yet he could have answered as Elgar did when asked how his music came into being: 'It's all around in the air. You reach out and take what you want.'

Brady's text for 1692 is vastly more sensible than Fishburn's for 1683, but it is the magnificent growth of *musical* conception, a grasp of large units and of the whole, that makes the 1692 'Hail, bright Cecilia' pre-eminent. Of all the odes this is the one that the reader is most likely to know, and a programme note from item to item is unnecessary. Brady offers very little visual imagery, but extols the birth and personality of musical instruments, including voices, singly and in ensemble. Purcell seizes the chance to deal with them almost as if they were dramatic characters. Thus at 'Hark, each Tree its silence breaks', the duettists represent the 'vocal' box and fir so that the bass (!) evokes 'the spritely violin' and the soprano the less actively beguiling flute:

Ex.19   St. Cecilia Ode, 1692

We note that there is no naive cadenza for either instrument. (No trumpet sounds in 'Sound the trumpet', the duet for two counter-tenors in 'Come ye sons of art' for Queen Mary's birthday in 1694.) The invitation to contrast the characters of instruments brings response in the splendid overture which, along with the Trumpet

Overture in *The Indian Queen*, we wish were used more often (if it is ever used already) as a concert overture. Even to ears accustomed to the rich sonorities of the romantic orchestra, such an effect as the change (between C and D in the list of movements given below and shown in Ex. 20) can be thrilling.

Overture to the 1692 Ode on St Cecilia's Day

A. D Major, Maestoso;[1] Dialogue between trumpets and strings with oboes. 10 bars.

B. D major, Allegro; canzona used again in the 1693 Queen Mary Ode. 36 bars.

C. A minor, Adagio; phrases alternating between strings and oboes. 48 bars.

D. (i) D major, Allegro in 3/8, featuring trumpets and drums prominently. 56 bars.

   (ii) D minor, Adagio in 4/4, for strings and oboes only. 6 bars.

   (iii) D major, Allegro. Repetition of D (i).

Ex.20

The promise of scale in this overture is fulfilled, not merely in length of choruses and other items, but in a sequence of keys destined to make a grand finale from the choruses-enclosing-'verse'-quartet, an uninterrupted sequence of movements which are now labelled nos. 13–15. There would have been no D major item between the overture and that climactic finale ('Hail, bright Cecilia, great Patroness of us and Harmony') if Purcell had not needed the trumpet key for no. 11, the counter-tenor solo 'The fife and all the harmony of war'. Led by a short bass solo, the opening chorus is in

[1] The Italian designations of movements are editorial.

D minor, its unanimous cries of 'Hail' coming brilliantly upon the second and fourth beats, after rests, the better to offset the fugal points beginning on the beat. Thereafter, with the exception just mentioned, the keys are related to D minor: A minor; F major ("Tis Nature's voice', the counter-tenor solo first sung by Purcell himself with 'incredible graces', surely not more elaborate than those written out); B flat for the tremendous chorus 'Soul of the world', also with that effective 'off-beat' entry; G minor for an oboe symphony leading to soprano solo and a chorus; C major for a verse trio; E minor for the bass solo 'Wondrous machine' – on a ground bass but shaped like an aria with neatly managed modulations to G major and B minor, and attractive interplay between singer and oboes. This is considered the best of many admirable solo items. The list need not be continued.

One might expect trumpets and drums to be used first in royal odes, but neither welcome songs nor birthday tributes engage them until 1690. They bring pomp to the Yorkshire Feast Song of 1689 and the ode for Trinity College, Dublin, of 1694. These commissions were undertaken during Purcell's years of best dramatic music but their near-Handelian grandeur does not seem highly inventive to ears fresh from that great 1692 St Cecilia ode. It is dangerous to call them conventional unless one names composers who established or shared the conventions. The chorus work alone brands them distinctively Purcellian, but not of best vintage. The same criticism might be expected after perusal of the royal odes purveyed in fulfilment of duty, often to verses of incredible poverty and hyperbole, of which the following (in a work well worth performing today) is one of the better samples.

> This point of time ends all, all your grief;
> In bringing Sacred Caesar it has brought relief.
> In his just praise your noblest songs let fall,
> And let 'em be immortal all,
> Immortal as the fame he's won,
> The wonders he's in battle done,
> In which he did not danger shun
> But made his name outlasting as the sun.

And so to a final chorus:

> While in music and verse our duty we show,
> And though we never can pay what we owe,
> Yet all we can raise,
> Our little, little mites we humbly throw
> Into the boundless treasury of their praise.

47

We suppose 'their praise' to refer to James II and his consort 'in whom does triumph each commanding grace, an angel's mien and a matchless face'. Within four years of this ode sacred Caesar was so unwelcome that his reign was terminated, yet none of the odes addressed to his predecessor were of the quality of those addressed to him, and we have no such work by Purcell directly addressed to his successor, William of Orange. This 1686 'Ye tuneful Muses', however, merits notice in a guide that cannot spare comment upon much that its readers are not likely to hear. We therefore exclude most of the royal odes from discussion in these pages, but wish that an occasional airing were given to their instrumental pieces, and to a few other items which would bear separation from context, such as the E minor tenor solo on a ground bass, 'From their serene and rapturous joys', in the last (1684) ode for Charles II.

Fortunately performances of 'Ye tuneful Muses' are furthered by the fact that Vaughan Williams prepared a handy vocal score[1] for a festival of English music which impressed musical scholars from overseas at Cambridge in 1933. The work is in Purcell's favourite basic G minor with a short but admirable slow-fast overture, followed by a lengthy complex of verse and chorus such as justified our grouping the last sections of the 1683 'Welcome to all the pleasures' as a finale. It is noteworthy that Vaughan Williams did not number the constituent items separately. No doubt he was attracted to the use, at the end of this opening group, both in the chorus and a following ritornello, of what he calls a folk dance, 'Hey boys, up go we'. It is in fact introduced first as a bass to the counter-tenor solo at 'Be lively then and gay', then transferred to the violins during the chorus as at Ex. 21. Purists may not agree that trumpets and drums, imitated for the symphony and chorus in C major – 'From the rattling of drums and the trumpet's loud sound' – may be actually used just in that middle section of the ode. It is a pity that the counter-tenor solo 'With him he brings the partner of his throne', on a ground that continues for a long ritornello, is unsuitable for separate performance.

Unlike some of the Queen Mary Odes, none of those for James II except 'Ye tuneful Muses' is scored for other instruments than strings with continuo, and that exception adds only two recorders. Its predecessor of 1685, 'Why are all the Muses mute?', has not been discussed. It is disappointing and unlikely to be generally revived;

[1] Novello, 1933.

Ex.21

Welcome Song, 1686

not so, however, the last of the three James II welcome songs, 'Sound the trumpet, beat the drum', of 1687. No less an artist than Gostling seems to have been available for some of the virtuoso bass solos. At its opening, counter-tenor and bass duly evoke the fanfare and paradiddle of their respective instruments before they are joined by the chorus in a broad, festive Handelian D major style. The following tenor solo is built on the ground bass quoted at Ex. 22 overleaf, but the ode (by repute – not often by performance) is remembered for another ground bass, the long instrumental chaconne which was later used in *King Arthur*.[1]

---

[1] The F major chaconne is printed as 'The Grand Dance' at the end of the Novello vocal score. It is effective in that position because *King Arthur* has two overtures, one in D minor and one in D major. It is known, however, that the chaconne was the 'First Music' and the D minor overture the 'Second Music' in the original production of *King Arthur*.

Ex.22

That semi-opera is again recalled in the second of the six birthday odes for Queen Mary (1690) which, as observed above, is the first 'royal' ode to incur trumpets and drums, for the 'symphony' in 'Arise my Muse' recurs in *King Arthur*. It was pointed out that King William was offered no welcome songs, but the 1690 birthday ode for Queen Mary pays tribute to his protection of the Anglican Church (called 'Eusebia') which laments his departure for the battlefield in a counter-tenor solo. Its close is quoted on several histories, not all by Englishmen, but we show it again at Ex. 23. The whole ode is well worth revival, if only for this counter-tenor solo and the dazzling splendour of its first chorus. There is also, as one expects, a fine duet on a ground bass. The 1691 ode is also fully scored but less attractive. The 1691 ode reverts to G minor and, to some extent, the style of the pre-trumpet works based on the verse anthem; it has elicited the notice of some writers because its soprano solo has for its bass a tune called 'Cold and raw' which was said to have pleased the queen. Trumpets and splendour return in 'Celebrate this festival', the 1693 ode, which begins with a C major version of the overture to the St Cecilia ode of 1692, and is worth revival; even so, it is unlikely to achieve the popularity of its successor, the last ode for the birthday of Queen Mary, 1694, 'Come ye sons of art'. (This is available in a vocal score edited by Tippett and Bergmann.[1]) The trumpets return, though only one during the overture, which is that first heard (i.e. beginning Act II in the play) before the masque in *The Indian Queen*. An oboe almost deceives the ear into supposing that the second trumpet is playing during the first two movements – *largo* and *allegro* (canzona) – which are followed by an *adagio* for strings on a slowly descending chromatic bass. There seems no other reason for its pathos but to make the alto invitation and chorus 'Come, come, ye sons of art, come, come away' sound all the merrier with the return to D major, and *two* trumpets.

The repeated 'come' was quoted deliberately. We might have quoted later repetitions – 'to celebrate, to celebrate this triumphant

[1] Schott, 1952.

Ex.23

Recorders

Queen Mary Ode, 1690

Continuo   Fate   must not, Fate   must not   let—him   go.   Fate

must not, no — must not, no   must not   let him   go.

day', 'sound, sound, sound the trumpet', 'Wake, wake, wake the harp', 'The day no common, no, no, no, no common festival should be'. These repetitions and the prolongation of such words as 'around', 'great', 'Im-mor—tal' and dozens of others were part of the means by which Purcell could bring into finely balanced phrases and sections of music the lines of poor verses which often failed to scan. Readers are surely familiar with the duet 'Sound the trumpet', with its 'On the sprightly oboe play', and may observe in it the technique of repetitions and 'runs'. (The range of altos or counter tenors in that duet is shown by the fact that it can be sung as a two-part ensemble by trebles or sopranos.) The practice may be illustrated (Ex. 24) from the bass solo which precedes the final jubilant duet-with-chorus.

Ex.24

Queen Mary Ode, 1694

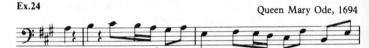

These, these, these are the sacred charms, these are the sacred charms that

shield   her   dar –   –   –   –   –   –   – ing

he - ro in___ the   field

Among the odes over which we have not lingered there are beautiful items which must be described as locked up in their contexts. They may very occasionally be heard but there is little hope of their coming into repertory. One hopes this will not long remain true of most of the ten exquisite and short secular cantatas (called by some scholars 'chamber cantatas') to words by Cowley and others. Most of them are duets or trios, but 'When night her purple veil' and some of the others need a Gostling! Most of them have admirable parts for violins or recorders. We show at Ex. 25 the opening of 'How pleasant is this flowery vale' of 1688, a duet for soprano and tenor accompanied by recorders and continuo. The chamber style of these works prevents their ever becoming, like the later odes with trumpets and drums, forerunners of the Handelian grand manner. Manfred Bukofzer, in *Music in the Baroque Era*, concludes his comments on Purcell with a paragraph beginning:

From the days of Burney until recently [1948] Purcell has been appraised largely in the light of what has come after him. Only the last phase of his

Ex.25

Secular cantata

Recorders

Cont.

development . . . has been taken to represent the 'real' Purcell . . . works of the early and middle periods . . . had to be forced into line by the notorious Victorian 'revisions'. Today a reversal of opinion has occurred. Works that seem to anticipate Handel hold less interest for us than the earlier ones in which the English idiom of the middle baroque reaches its consummation.

This is true as applied to many of the odes; even more important is our discrimination between those which seem to have been completed hurriedly, have good items but are unremarkable as whole conceptions, and those which quiver throughout with a life that betokens joy in their making.

Theatre and Dramatic Music

Purcell was the first Englishman whose London theatre songs reached provincial ears without arrangement for keyboard. Unlike his church music, much of his music for the stage was published while he lived; more was disseminated soon after he died, for Playford included it in the tribute to Purcell called *Orpheus Britannicus*, the popularity of which elicited a second and third edition. Plagued by panatropes which bring commercial city music into rural inns, we do not readily imagine an agricultural England (most men at Trafalgar and Waterloo came from villages) wherein music was 'folk and traditional' – a modern phrase which wisely avoids discrimination; yet fifty years after Purcell's death Charles Wesley sought hearty singing of 'Love divine, all loves excelling' by fitting his verses to the melody of Purcell's 'Fairest Isle'.

People from the provinces must sometimes have sampled London shows and heard Purcell's songs and dances, but historians declare that many, though royalist, still disapproved of the theatre, and not all were humble folk. The Restoration comedies which satirised vice and folly were thought by the unsophisticated to reflect the general morality of court and society, who comprised the bulk of London theatre-goers. The extent of their 'permissiveness' cannot fairly be judged by coarse plays, but their delight in music offered during the plays can be surmised by the evidence of its separate publication. Purcell had supplied music for nearly a dozen plays before the great series of dramatic works now remembered chiefly through his contribution. These belong to his last six years. Among them only *Dido and Aeneas* can be called an opera, if that is the exclusive designation of a *dramma per musica*. The others are conveniently called operas, semi-opera, or dialogue-operas, for nobody is likely to compare them with those nineteenth-century French lyric dramas which, however serious, were classified under the general title *opéra comique* and denied production at the Opéra because they contained spoken passages. The list of what shall here be called Purcell's operas follows.

1689 *Dido and Aeneas*. Libretto by the poet laureate, Nahum Tate. Performed at Josias Priest's school in Chelsea.

1690 *Dioclesian*. Music for *The Prophetess, or the History of Dioclesian*, adapted by Betterton from Beaumont and Fletcher. The pastoral masque in the last act, often sung separately, was enthusiastically received

and the score was published in 1691, whereas only a few songs from
Dido and Aeneas were published.

1691 *King Arthur, or The British Worthy*. Libretto prepared by Dryden.

1692 *The Fairy Queen*. Play by Elkanah Settle. Shakespeare's supply of
ideas from *A Midsummer Night's Dream* is almost unrecognisable
in a music-dominated spectacle with such masque personages as
monkeys, nymphs, shepherds and Chinamen. Some items from this
work – Purcell's longest theatre score – were published.

1695 *The Indian Queen*. Adapted from a tragedy by Dryden and Sir Robert
Howard. The music is most continuous for a masque in Act II.
Another masque with music by Daniel Purcell, Henry's brother,
may have been used for the first performance but is more likely to
have been added for a 1696 revival. *The Indian Queen* was pirated
with a flattering address to the composer!

1695 *The Tempest, or The Enchanted Island*. Adapted from Shakespeare by
Shadwell, who kept the main characters but added masque personages such as Neptune, Amphitrite, devils and tritons.

A brief review of the previous association of music with drama in
England is desirable, though we need not go back to medieval
plays or the Elizabethan delight in songs within plays when female
parts were taken by choristers. Masques, lavishly costumed and
staged for royal and aristocratic pleasure, spread from Italy to
France, and thence to England where, between 1605 and 1631,
Ben Jonson was privileged to devise them for the Stuart court.[1]
Their allegorical and mythological subjects were presented with
vocal and instrumental music and spoken verse. Greatly relished
were surprising entries of masquers or dancers in fancy costume –
from a shell, grotto, chariot, descending cloud and so on. Like
operatic *intermezzi*, Jonson's anti-masques with Inigo Jones's
scenery added comic or grotesque elements such as animals,
spectres, dolphins, 'Indians' and satyrs. The witches and sailors in
Dido and Aeneas are in this tradition, and recent knowledge shows
that the building suited it. The courtyard of Priest's school had
cloisters on one side with passages leading to a timber yard. From
their arcading the witches could issue and maybe give 'In our deep
vaulted cell' a more realistic echo than the 'composed' one; the
sailors could 'take a bowsy short leave of their nymphs on the shore'

---

[1] More than sixty choral, vocal and instrumental pieces can be inspected
in a handy volume, *Songs and Dances from the Stuart Masque*, collected by
Andrew Sabol. Brown University Press, Providence, Rhode Island, 1965.
(Via O.U.P.)

and dance their hornpipe where masts and sails made the yard beyond the passages into an imaginary quay.

When the theatres were closed in 1642, private productions in houses and schools were not forbidden. Milton's *Comus* at Ludlow, with music by Henry Lawes, was as far removed from the extravagant court masque as from Italian opera; it may have helped to commend dramatic performances as educational and morally improving. In 1659 Parliament itself promoted Shirley's *Cupid and Death* as a 'private entertainment' for the Portuguese ambassador. Passages in recitative had been used by William Lawes and Lanier, who did not exclude spoken dialogue; that daring step was taken by musicians personally known to Purcell after Davenant, Evelyn and others had returned from Italy extolling the wonders of opera. Locke was one of five contributors to Davenant's *The Siege of Rhodes*, given at Rutland House in 1656. It was repeated after the Restoration, but Dryden declares in the preface to *The Conquest of Granada* that 'Davenant review'd his *Siege of Rhodes* and caus'd it to be acted as a just drama'. The original music has been lost. Locke wrote music for other plays at such continuous length that one might imagine some of it to belong to fully-fledged opera in English, the whole text set to music, but of true opera we can at present examine only one specimen before Purcell's. This is Blow's *Venus and Adonis* of 1682, a delightful short chamber opera, yet called 'A Masque for the entertainment of the King'. Well known for its amusing passages, such as the spelling lesson for the Little Cupids, it ceases to be a pastoral comedy at the end, when the wounded Adonis returns from the hunt to be mourned by Venus and an impressive chorus worthy of Purcell himself.

DIDO AND AENEAS

As measured by the clock, this also is a chamber opera, yet one which German musicographers have called 'Shakesperian' because the main characters are so impressively real and human. It is equally remarkable that a Frenchman, Romain Rolland, should speak of the 'perfection' of *Dido and Aeneas*. Why comment on these opinions? Because one who hears the work for the first time, despite admiration of almost every bar of the music, may wonder why the scenes change so rapidly, or why a plot which moved the composer to such rich emotion is kept within a frame too small to fill an evening's programme. The wish that scenes changed more quickly and that action were swifter comes in later operas when the music seems extra to the drama, delaying it instead of carrying it forward. Great Purcell as much as great Wagner or Verdi answers the question: 'Why maintain the spell of music at all in drama?' The answer is simpler than many theorists think. Because it *prolongs* what is dramatically important in some situations better than words can. In a spoken play Dido's lament could not extend to Purcell's heavenly length. Such rhetoric as 'Why did he leave me? What shall I do?' might risk unwelcome replies from the audience. Blank verse might express her grief at acceptable length, but the music does so more effectively than the finest conceivable soliloquy, and the emotion is extended by the final chorus 'With drooping wings'.

Action, not drama, is static when music carries the drama. If the drama did not live within the music for most of *Tristan and Isolde* we should fidget while waiting for the few visual happenings – King Mark's return or the sight of Isolde's ship on the way to the dying Tristan. We indeed wish that *Dido and Aeneas* were a full-length opera, and that more often the situations were prolonged by such fine music; but we may well wonder that a work written to be enacted in the courtyard of a 'society' school, deliberately cast for the pupils and timed to be no longer than a 'Speech Day' ceremony, should so often make us feel that we are witnessing a work of greater scale rather than an ambitious chamber opera. We may also wonder why the constriction (in time and space) is so rarely evident as we listen – in short, to echo Rolland, that despite the scanty precedents in England for complete *dramma per musica* so much here approaches perfection.

If we disregard the contributions of the witches and sailors – the masque elements no doubt most enjoyed by the young ladies and by Priest, who was a dancing master and choreographer of repute – we shall see that Nahum Tate, like many other librettists of successful operas, presented Vergil's story straightforwardly even if the language is sometimes absurd. The fault is not often obvious during the singing except during recitative:

> Thus on the fatal bank of Nile
> Weeps the deceitful crocodile.
> Thus hypocrites, who murder act,
> Make Heaven and Fate the authors of the fact.

The important truth is that Tate and Purcell seemed to understand the kind of situations that can be well served by music and the kind that cannot. The copy preserved in the Royal College of Music, London, shows that Tate wrote a prologue for Phoebus, Venus and such beings as nereids and nymphs. Understandably, however, it is rarely if ever used; nor has it been suggested that Purcell set any of it. The dramatic unity of the main plot is ensured by a minor-key overture, leading immediately to Dido's pathetic confession of her love, and the thread of that tragic emotion is unharmed by the anti-masque scenes for the witches and sailors; we are even aware of it during the very masculine and extrovert music sung by Aeneas as he boasts his triumph in the hunt. The extensive use of chorus, participating as in Greek tragedy or in some of Gluck's operas, is also a strongly unifying force.

DIOCLESIAN

The music for *Dioclesian* brought its composer the greatest acclaim he had received, for it had more admirers than could have been well acquainted with his church or chamber music or his opera given at a school. Priest, the proprietor of that school, being frequently engaged by London theatres, is likely to have directed the choreography for the fauns, nymphs, shepherds and followers of Bacchus, Flora, Silvanus, etc. in this dazzling *Dioclesian*.[1] The greatest magnificence was reserved subtly for the last act with its masque: 'A machine descends, so large it fills the space from the frontispiece of the stage to the farther end of the house . . . In it are four several stages representing the palaces of two gods and two goddesses . . .'

The elaborate scene transformations invite the question: 'What have these contrivances, personages and spectacles to do with the history, albeit the fictional history, of a Roman emperor?' Nothing at all. The prophetess of the sub-title foretells the rise to imperial power of the soldier Diocles, already hailed by the army. His authority is not assured until his victory over the Persians and in a courtship that, of course, does not run smoothly. The masque for his entertainment as the new Caesar is ordered by the lady who has successfully exposed a plot to assassinate him.

As in the rest of the semi-operas these main characters act the play and speak their parts. The fantastic and gorgeous scenes

[1] The Dorset Garden theatre certainly retained Priest's services for several years.

employ a larger troupe which has to include selected singers and dancers, and for most of us 'Purcell's *Dioclesian*' means the music for the Act V masque which needs not a word from the main plot. We cannot be blamed for performing it on its own as the splendid entity it is, and which Purcell himself published in this form, for even today it alone is available in a handy vocal score. Yet fine music comes in other junctures of the play, as readers will recognise if they know the song 'What shall I do to show how much I love her?' or, if they consult the Purcell Society edition, the overture (or 'First Music' to the play), the first chorus, or the Act III Chaconne, wherein two flutes play in canon.

'Orchestration' seems a pretentious term to apply to Lully's or Purcell's treatment of a basic strings-with-continuo ensemble to which they sometimes added recorders and/or oboes, sometimes a trumpet or two trumpets and drums; yet in the emergent orchestra as we know it any contrasting of timbres, even tremolo, pizzicato effects within the strings alone or a temporary resting of certain instruments, can be accurately regarded as belonging to the early stages of the art of orchestration. An advance in this contrast of timbres seems evident from *Dioclesian* onwards. If space allowed one might quote both 'vocal scoring' and contrasts between voices and instruments from that first decidedly 'Handelian' chorus of the play, 'Sing Ios!' Instead Ex. 26 is a short passage that contrasts three instrumental textures during the trio and chorus 'Triumph victori- ous Love', the final piece in the Masque. From the same piece we might also quote examples of contrasts within the vocal texture. It is not easy to say why music that is simpler and more conventional contains one of the most thrilling passages in the whole of *Dioclesian*; it is the opening of the Masque – a short prelude during which

Ex.26   Dioclesian

Cupid enters and calls the 'Nymphs and the fauns from the woods, the naiads and gods of the floods' (Ex. 27).

KING ARTHUR, OR THE BRITISH WORTHY

Who promulgated the selection of the 'Nine Worthies' (and why there are nine) the author cannot discover. They begin with classical and Jewish heroes (Hector, Alexander, King David) and finish with Charlemagne. Britain claims only Arthur among the nine. As we should expect, this Dryden–Purcell extravaganza appealed to 'British' patriotism among spectators more likely to have Saxon than British blood in their veins. What matter that the story shows how, after many a previous affray against Oswald, King of Kent, the British Worthy wins a last battle and magnanimously allows the Saxon invader to leave the island? Success is advanced by Merlin's supernatural powers, but Oswald also has his magician, whose sprites are to 'harass the Britons and lead them into bogs'. Merlin induces one of them to change sides. He also guides the love plot, for Arthur and Oswald are rivals for Emmeline, blind daughter of the Duke of Cornwall. She is captured and shown the Frost Scene to display the powers at Oswald's command. After she has been duly rescued and her sight restored, Merlin becomes the prophet of Britain's glory, shown in scenes of Arcadian health, wealth and love-making, all eclipsed by the final patriotic tableau – the Order of St George and the Garter.

Apart from the Frost Scene no masque is deliberately introduced as it was in *Dioclesian*, yet every act pays tribute to the masque tradition.

Act I 'The scene represents the Saxon camp. Three gods, Woden, Thor and Freya, are placed on pedestals. In front are ranged three soldiers, voluntary victims to the deities.'

Battle Symphony. British song and chorus of victory, 'Come if you dare'.

Act II   The sprite Philidel laments the slaughter. Merlin descends 'in a chariot drawn by dragons'. Spirits attempt to lead the Britons astray with 'Hither this way' but are thwarted by Merlin's spirits. Songs of shepherds and shepherdesses. Hornpipe.

Act III   'Osmond strikes the ground with his wand. The scene changes to a winter prospect.' Shivering songs and choruses cease when Cupid dispels winter with the warmth of love. Another hornpipe.

Act IV   'Arthur in the Enchanted Wood is beguiled by sirens who rise from the stream.'

Act V   'The British Ocean in a storm. Aeolus in a cloud above . . . the winds disperse . . . Britannia rises from the waters.'

Now Lully had a frost scene in *Isis*, and even before Rameau's genius exulted in fantastic ballets and scenes known as *divertissements*, such things were enjoyed in so-called *tragédies lyriques*. The difference between the French and the English conception is that all the text is sung in French opera, whereas Arthur, Oswald, Emmeline and the magicians do not sing even if present during a musical scene.

French opera did not produce harmony and counterpoint of Purcell's skill or daring. How the *tremolando* was performed in the Frost Scene is unimportant; it had been used by Monteverdi and others, and we imagine it more effective (in evoking shivering cold) from a few hard-toned muted violins than from a large, rich ensemble. Today it would be no more realistic than the galloping horse in Monteverdi's *Tancredi and Clorinda* but for the harmonies, including whole-tone progressions:

Ex.28

Great though Rameau's invention is, especially in dances, we rate Purcell's melodic invention above that of any French composer before Berlioz, yet it is unlikely that Purcell conceived melody without its harmony and circumstances. The melodic ideas in *King Arthur* are particularly satisfying when words and situation are not of a kind previously presented to him. Thus *good* Purcell is found in the overtures and the Saxon sacrificial scene, but strikingly *original* Purcell follows when the beguiling sprites, later the sirens, stimulate his imagination to atmospheric effect.

The final act still deeply moves English audiences when they have the rare opportunity of seeing *King Arthur* staged. Some of Dryden's verses would do that poet no great honour in anthologies; some would sound comical if we merely read them; but *King Arthur* was the first play deliberately written for Purcell's music – and by a Poet Laureate who admitted his conversion to 'opera'. The text is rarely great Dryden, but undoubtedly it 'sings' well. One might expect musico-literary bombast to make the last patriotic spectacle seem as dated as are the Quinault–Lully pomposities addressed to Louis before and after lyric dramas. In fact Dryden makes no mention of empire. The Order of the Garter provided visual pomp, but the libretto and music chiefly express affection, not pride. Comus and Peasants sing 'Your hay it is mown and your corn is reaped . . . and merrily roar out harvest home' to something suggesting folk-song origin but ending 'And hey for the honour of old England'. Then Venus comes forward with 'Fairest Isle' which, in the theatre, can bring one strangely near to tears. A love dialogue between a nymph and a shepherd covers preparation of the grand finale ('*Scene: The Order of the Garter*'), introduced by 'Trumpet Tune'. Considering the period, can we regard what follows as bombastically chauvinistic? The song is sung by Honour:

> Saint George, the Patron of our Isle, a soldier and a Saint,
> On that auspicious order smile, which love and arms will plant.

Chorus:

> Our natives not alone appear to court this martial prize,
> But foreign kings, adopted here, their crowns at home despise.
> Our sov'reign high in awful state his honours shall bestow,
> And see his sceptred subjects wait on his commands below.

Then the 'Grand Dance' – chaconne.

Downes in *Roscius Anglicanus* (1708), having declared that '*King Arthur*, an opera wrote by Mr. Dryden, was excellently adorn'd with scenes and machines; the musical part set by famous Mr. Henry Purcel, and dances made by Mr. Jo. Priest. The play and musick pleas'd the Court and City, and being well perform'd, 'twas very gainful to the company.' The last sentence is remarkable since the production must have been costly, yet *King Arthur* was frequently revived in the eighteenth century and later. Garrick, Kemble, Mrs Siddons, Macready and even Irving produced it. Most of the other Purcell semi-operas were also produced long after the composer's death, though whether they were well treated or mauled one cannot say. In any case we cannot even now discover, from manuscripts of the work or from such anthologies as *Ayres for the Theatre*, the complete music of *King Arthur*. Most of us are happy enough with what was put together by Cummings in 1897, and a discussion of sources would be inappropriate here. One must, however, hope that readers may see the work staged, so impressive is the music in more than a merely musical context.

THE FAIRY QUEEN

In this largest of his dramatic scores

Purcell did not set a single line of Shakespeare.[1] The text he set consisted of ... short masques at the end of each of the five acts. The relationship with the [Shakespeare] play was mainly through Titania and her attendant fairies, hence the title. Ideally *The Fairy Queen* should be performed on the stage with both musical and dramatic components ... an elaborate and lengthy enterprise which need not be the only method of presenting this seventeenth-century masterpiece. For the music by itself is very well suited to a concert performance, particularly if a narrator is used to set the scene from time to time. The context of each section of the music is given in the Purcell Society Edition.

One heartily agrees with what has been quoted from Sir Anthony Lewis's preface to the 1966 revision of Novello's vocal score. It can be patronising to give spoken clues that spoil musical wit just as explaining spoils a joke. A narrator is an otiose and vulgar modern adjunct to *Le Carnaval des Animaux*, but Purcell's music emerges each time from spoken drama. In one or two splendid broadcasts of *The Fairy Queen* the BBC narrator has provided the elucidating connections briefly and neatly. Incidentally one may

[1] A remarkable fact, since he set 'Come unto these yellow sands' and 'Full fathom five' in Shadwell's adaptation from *The Tempest*. We may well wonder why Shadwell did not ask Purcell to set certain excerpts from *A Midsummer Night's Dream*, such as 'You spotted snakes' (lullaby for Titania) or Puck's envoi 'If we shadows have offended'. The song 'If music be the food of love, sing on' uses only that one line of Orsino's opening words from *Twelfth Night*, and then alters 'play on' to 'sing on'.

mention that to entrust the editing or the conducting of this work to the Principal of the Royal Academy of Music is peculiarly appropriate, since its library owns the manuscript almost certainly used for the original performance in 1692 and for revivals in the following year, several items being incontestably in Purcell's own handwriting. A few songs were added for the revival.

The work was an immense popular success, and no doubt Purcell would have published more of its music but for demands that he lacked time to fulfil. It is most likely that today's radio listeners would vote *The Fairy Queen* their favourite, if all five of Purcell's 'operas' (i.e. without *Dido and Aeneas*) were presented to them without the stage action. It calls for little or nothing in the composer's pathetic or sombre veins and, as we should expect, the very finest samples of his theatre music are chosen from the last he composed – from *The Indian Queen* and *The Tempest*; yet the level of verve, rhythmic invention and melodic allure is nowhere maintained by Purcell as extensively as in *The Fairy Queen*. Melody, more than other features of musical texture, has the widest appeal, and is worth considering here.

A tune is a 'catchy' melody; yet the most naive listeners may relish a melody which is too long for them to sing or whistle after only one or two hearings. The point is illustrated by Ex. 29, the 'Rondeau' in the 'Second Music' before the curtain, and Ex. 30, the Hornpipe from the 'First Music', which begins as a tune but is marvellously extended to be less easily remembered but maybe more admired than Ex. 29 (see overleaf). The same may be said of Ex. 31, although it seems to be inspired (as are other pastoral items in this work) by folksong or dance. Many of these enchanting tunes are instrumental, within a profusion of dances or other short pieces which cover movements of machines, stage properties or personages. We shall observe later that most of the famous songs are florid and truly operatic in the Italian aria or concerto style.

Every one of the five acts, either with Titania's fairies or with 'masque' characters, gave rein to Purcell's obvious delight in colour, wit and fantasy.

Act I   Titania's fairies tease a drunken poet, whose 'Fi-fi-fi-fill up the bowl', 'I'm a scu-scu-scurvy knave' and other bass stutterings are deliciously answered by the soprano fairies – 'Pinch him, pinch him for his crimes; pinch him for his dogg'rel rhymes'.

Act II   The fairies call on the birds to join them. After an 'echo' chorus

Ex.29

Ex.30

Ex.31

etc.

and symphony comes the 'Entrance of Night, Mystery, Secrecy and Sleep, with their attendants'. Violins and violas are muted, cellos and basses silenced. The upper strings play in canon about Night's aria, and a 'Dance for the Followers of Night' (a canon 4-in-2!), Ex. 32 (p. 70), follows the whispered 'Sleep Chorus'. This whole section is an expressive as well as a technical *tour de force*.

Act III Titania demands the transformation of 'this place' to an enchanted lake, and arranges an entertainment for Bottom, including a

'Symphony while the Swans come forward' and dances for the Fairies, the Green Men and the Haymakers between songs and a beautiful 'Dialogue for Corydon and Mopsa'. This masque ends with a general hornpipe.

Act IV A pageant of the seasons follows the 'chasing away' of Night and Winter after the entry of Phoebus and the chorus 'Hail great Parent!' A five-movement grand overture opens this act with timpani and trumpets and is followed by the festive duet, 'Let the fifes and the clarions and shrill trumpets sound'. Then follows the chorus, 'Hail great parent!', after which a pageant of the seasons ensues. Contrasting minor-key arias for Autumn ('See, see my many-coloured fields') and Winter ('Now Winter comes slowly, pale, meagre and old'), with Purcellian indulgence in chromatics, are banished when the chorus again exults in 'Hail great Parent!' and a gavotte-like fourth-act tune brings down the curtain.

Act V Titania orders a Masque of Hymen. The prelude and solo Epithalamium ('Thrice happy lovers') lead to 'The Plaint' – of a lover who despairs that she shall 'ever see him more'. Was this lament over a ground bass (like that of Dido's lament) included because such things were popular, or as a foil to the brilliance to follow? The final numbers include 'Hark how all things with one sound rejoice', 'Hark the echoing air a triumph sings', a Chinese scene, a dance for six Monkeys, a duet, a trio and the Grand Chaconne.

No quotation from the two brilliant solos first mentioned among the final numbers of Act V is made here, not only because they are likely to be widely known and are often sung in recitals, but also because their significance in Purcell's development lies in their complete form. Like several other items in *The Fairy Queen* they approach the *aria d'agilità*. Italians and others brought enough music to London for Purcell to know arias by composers contemporary with Monteverdi's disciples, Cavalli and Cesti, and possibly some by Alessandro Scarlatti. Many were sung by G. F. Grossi, called 'Siface', a castrato employed in James II's chapel and sufficiently admired elsewhere in London for Purcell to include among his harpsichord pieces one in D minor called *Sifauchi's Farewell*. Purcell's florid arias, such as 'Hark the echoing air', with preludes, repeated motto phrases, and final references to opening ideas, rarely resemble exactly the Scarlatti–Handel *da capo* designs which framed the voice with ritornelli in a symmetrical key-scheme so that the substitution of an instrumentalist for a singer would produce a concerto movement. Purcell's textures (such as the oboes and bassoon accompaniment to the Aerial Spirits in *The Indian Queen*) are often concerto-like, but his 'airs', as he called them, are more unpredictable than high baroque arias, even to his combining an Italianate form with a ground bass.

The demands from singers in *The Fairy Queen* and subsequent dramatic works indicate the availability of fine artists even in the choruses. Purcell's orchestra must also have included leaders of high calibre and others nimble with their bows if we may judge from changes of style required for consecutive ideas. Among the attractions of *The Fairy Queen* are many dances with rhythms that have no French counterparts even in the Rameau treasury.

THE INDIAN QUEEN

Unlike other Purcell 'operas' *The Indian Queen* was first produced not at Dorset Garden but the Theatre Royal on the site of the present Drury Lane Theatre. One approaches Purcell's greatest dramatic music with two regrets: that his last two 'operas' use much less music than the former two, and that listeners have had few opportunities to hear more than single items from them, such as the Trumpet Overture, or 'I attempt from love's sickness to fly'. Recordings are badly needed: some readers are no doubt fortunate enough still to possess the Record Society's long-playing disc of *The Indian Queen* (this was made in France and admirably directed by Anthony Bernard).

The background of *The Indian Queen* is a war between Peru and Mexico. Having defeated Acacis, the Mexican general, young Montezuma is asked by the Inca to choose his reward. His request for the Inca's daughter, Orazia, is refused as presumptuous, so Montezuma deserts to the Mexicans, only to find himself the object of their queen's infatuation. She (Zempoalla) consults Ismeron, her priest-magician, whose incantations ('Ye twice ten hundred deities') conjure up various spirits, including the God of Dreams. The beautiful solo with what Lully called the *concert d'oubuoès* foretells no respite – 'Seek not to know what must not be revealed'. After her charming 'I attempt from love's sickness to fly' her mood changes to rage. She will fire Ismeron's temple and, having imprisoned the Inca and Orazia, has them brought with Montezuma for sacrifice in the Temple of the Sun, 'all of gold, with four priests in habits of white and red feathers attending a bloody altar'. Acacis is first killed for attempting a rescue, but the grisly rites are halted by news of a revolution (frequent in that part of the globe!) in which Montezuma has been proclaimed king. He takes Orazia for his queen; Zempoalla stabs herself, and the Inca is free, presumably to go home.

We cannot always tell why certain parts of these plays and not others are chosen for the music, nor do we know if Dryden and Howard or Purcell himself suggested what he should compose. We expect the First Music, Second Music and Overture, but immediately after them comes a lively duet between an Indian boy and the girl Quivera. He bids her wake and flee from a place that is shortly to become a battlefield – a strange pastoral introduction to a spoken act dealing with bloodshed. The second act brings music in the grand manner praising Her Mexican Majesty – a fine overture (the one for 'Come ye sons of art' of 1694 transposed down into key C), then a masque for Zempoalla in which the soloists are Fame and Envy. Fame's martial song 'We come to sing great Zempoalla's glory' is later repeated by orchestra and chorus, and by the time we have heard each of its two strophes several times (as with 'See the conquering hero comes') we feel that, grand though it is, Envy's contrasting bass solo is more interesting – 'What flatt'ring noise is thissss that makes my snakes all hissss'. Envy's troupe of attendants joins 'this' and 'hiss' with comic onomatopoeic effect.

Of extraordinary beauty are the contributions to Act III, beginning with Ismeron's 'Ye twice ten hundred deities' and the duet of the spirits 'How happy are we' followed by their chorus 'Cease to languish then in vain'. The concluding tune of this act is a rondo, one of the most charming of Purcell's instrumental pieces. Passages of spoken dialogue occur between these numbers and one cannot but regret that the whole act was not set to music, in anticipation of Rameau's great incantation scene with the magician Ismenor in *Dardanus*. The sacrificial scene, being cut short by the messenger with news of the revolution, brings only a solemn antiphonal chorus, but a very fine one. Before it, however, in the previous act comes that song which one might select as among the most lovely ever composed, though its structure is as simple as Blow's 'The Self Banished'. It is to the words 'They tell us that you mighty powers above make perfect your joy and your blessings by love. Ah! why do you suffer?' Nothing but the melody is quoted at Ex. 32 in order to show how, by the vocal line alone, intensity can

Ex.32

Air: The Indian Queen, Act 4

be consistently increased. We hear Purcell praised for choral splendour, for recitative-like declamation, for mastery of counterpoint, for being both conservative and radical in harmony, yet Purcellians tend to treasure one or two works in which they imagine the quintessence of their hero's genius to be enshrined. One devotee would forgo all the grandeur and declamation to keep just this song.

It is difficult not to suppose that Dryden and Howard hoped that Purcell would compose a final Masque of Hymen, and that he either thought it unnecessary or was too burdened with work. He had no compunction in re-serving an overture, and could have compiled a final masque from some of his previous theatre music or even odes. His brother's music for the finale, especially the vigorous first item, is perhaps too heavily depreciated by some critics who are wise after the event in knowing who supplied it; to be fair to them one admits that Daniel's professional competence, which church choirs know if 'D. Purcell in D minor' is still sung, is handicapped by its proximity to such a wealth of Henry's originality.

THE TEMPEST

When he published his music for a 1694 production of *The Tempest* and another of Shadwell's confections Locke declared that 'more has been done by me than any other' to introduce 'opera to England'. With characteristic spleen he tried to disarm criticism by forestalling it. 'The extreme Compass' of some of the parts did not concern a composer who was not 'like a Botching Stult, who being obliged to make habits for men cuts them for children'. It would be interesting to know his opinion of the music by Purcell commissioned for the 1695 revival. Locke had not been the only contributory composer to the earlier production, and therefore Westrup is able to show by fascinating quotations a comparison between the setting of 'Arise, ye subterranean winds' by Pietro Reggio and the famous one by Purcell.[1]

If quotations were made here only to whet appetites one could pick them blindfold from any page of the score. The only two (Exx. 33 and 34 overleaf) are chosen to show how closely as he approached his death Purcell anticipated the high Baroque style consolidated in Italy but associated here with Handel. That beginning of a chorus at Ex. 33 might be passed off as by Handel, but the whole piece from which it is taken could not. The chorus replies to two devils who ask 'Where does the black fiend Ambition reside?' Holst and some other musicians of his generation, who were rightly keen to make better known our English musical treasury, regretted Purcell's 'capitulation' to international forms and formulae, and much preferred his string fantasias and sonatas. He had far too strong a personality to lose by the supposed capitulation. So also had Handel, except when forced to compose too much and too fast. The trend of Purcell's ideals towards such forms as the Scarlattian aria is certainly evident, and is illustrated by the skeleton opening (Ex. 34) of an aria which actually bears the direction *da capo* after a middle section in triple tempo finishing in the dominant.

With no preceding First and Second Music *The Tempest* has a short but very fine overture for strings. It is missing from the authentic copies but was found in the library of the Royal College of Music in a manuscript headed 'Overture in Mr. P's Opera' and signed 'Mr. H. Purcell'. As it does not belong to any of the other 'operas' and is so intrinsically admirable one cannot question its inclusion in the score by Dent.

The first act is spoken. Music begins at the third scene of Act II – 'A Wild Island'. Downes described the earlier *Tempest* at Dorset

[1] J. A. Westrup, *Purcell*, The Master Musicians Series, Dent, 1965, pp. 145–6.

PURCELL

Ex.33

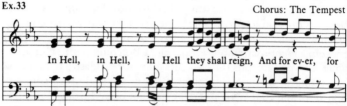

In Hell, in Hell, in Hell they shall reign, And for ev-er, for

ev - er, and for ev - er shall suf - fer the pain. In

Ex.34

Da capo aria

to four more bars

[Aeolus]

Come down, ____ come down, ____ come down ____ my ____

blus - ter-ers.

Come down, ____ come down, ____ come

Garden as 'made into an opera by Mr. Shadwell and having all new in it, as scenes and machines painted with myriads of aerial spirits, a table furnished with fruits, sweetmeats and all sorts of viands flying away just when Duke Trinculo and his companions were going to dinner'. That explains the Devils of Ex. 33 and the great aria 'Arise, ye subterranean winds', followed by a dance for the winds. (Purcell *must* have been pressed for time, for he boldly took this dance from *Cadmus et Hermione*, Lully's first opera, which had been produced in London.) Act III brings the lovely solos by Ariel which enchant Ferdinand. The first two, 'Come unto these yellow sands' and 'Full fathom five', finish with choruses, but they are not alone in losing much when they are heard only as single recital songs without their dramatic context. They are followed by 'Dry those eyes', with its masterly combination of ritornello-aria and ground bass, and the very Handelian 'Kind Fortune smiles'. The Devils return with a dance opening Act III which has only one other musical item, Dorinda's 'Dear pretty youth'. As we expect, Act V has the culminating splendour, a masque-like complex too long to be called a *scena* yet containing recitatives, airs and choruses. Its personages are Neptune, Amphitrite, Aeolus, Nereids and Tritons. There is no final chaconne nor is any dance included in the manuscripts, but it is difficult to believe that the choreographer's arts were not requisitioned for this spectacular finale. Perhaps a ballet was arranged to music from other plays.

It has been asked why in *The Fairy Queen* and *The Tempest* Purcell was not offered a libretto that allowed him to set more of Shakespeare's own words, including speeches by the principal characters. Mendelssohn helps us to find an explanation. It is true that the final (Berlin) compilation of his incidental music for *A Midsummer Night's Dream* includes a duet-setting of 'You spotted snakes' and a 'Melodrama and March of Elves' – the latter not specified by Shakespeare. They are rarely heard, and Mendelssohn's exquisite score includes no treatments of 'speeches', though many in the play are lyrical. No great play should be used as an opera libretto without such services as Boito's for Verdi. This is not only because music needs time to develop and be effective, but also because it is powerless to express what is conveyed by certain conjunctions (for instance, '*While* this happened . . .'). Many a bad libretto has included narrative instead of a series of situations. Whether a comedy like *Figaro* or a tragedy like *Boris Godunov*, great opera treats a story with continuous stop-go, its most memorable music drawing the mood or emotion from situations that can be explicit without narrative. Mussorgsky called his masterpiece a series of 'pictures'. Purcell was not frustrated by narrative, nor compelled to use tedious lengths of recitative; such recitative as he chose to use was powerfully effective. The spoken parts advanced the story, and if within it there were not enough opportunities for the contributions music can make more powerfully than words, either he or his 'librettists' shamelessly invented them.

To blame commercial theatres for neglect of Purcell's operas is unreasonable. We do not know what the participants in them were paid, nor to what extent producers could secure help from royal servants and court musicians; but certainly the size and appointments of Restoration stages, choruses, orchestras, and facilities for carpenters, etc. are not to be compared with those in modern opera houses. Consider only one detail, well described by Dennis Arundell in a programme note to a Cambridge *Dioclesian*. He writes about visual illusion:

Dramatic surprise was aided rather than hindered by the use of candlelight throwing direct, reflected or concealed radiance with colour on to cleverly painted scenery, which gave an impression of solid grandeur or dark mystery that nowadays is difficult to achieve in spite of modern devices. Highly ornamented costumes were needed to make the chief actors prominent. The scenes painted in the flat secured an impression of solid reality better than do modern solid sets with lighting that easily shows up their unreality. Great distance was suggested by subtle perspective. . . . It was heightened at the end of *Dioclesian* by entries, each further from the audience, by successively less tall performers – big men, ordinary men and women, youths, boys and girls, finally children at the farthest depth of the stage.

The length of 'run' and declarations that good profits were made show that expense could not deter producers from giving crowded houses (that is a few hundreds, not thousands) a new dramatic thrill, which also explains the immediate building of new opera houses or converting of theatres to opera after 1637 in Venice, when the San Cassiano Theatre provided for *the public* what had formerly been only for princes and the wealthy, who could afford it privately. Into London's spoken plays the Restoration theatre first brought the marvels of the former court masques.

Production of Purcell's operas in the average London theatre today incurs the cost of the following:

(i) Actors, paid union rates, so well trained that they avoid sudden reactions from imagination to ridicule when they declaim phraseology which, among many listeners today, sounds stilted and artificial while Shakespeare's does not.

(ii) A versatile and highly professional chorus, preferably of young voices.

(iii) An orchestra of rather more strings (but the same extra wind instruments) than were needed in Purcell's much smaller theatres.

(iv) Solo singers innocent of wobbling, swooping, gulching and technics used to disguise modern disinclination to train for the achievement of *bel canto*, i.e. perfect intonation, whatever the intervals, and perfect breath control in the moulding of phrases. The soloists include counter-tenors.

(v) Dancers, solo and *corps de ballet*.

Yet today we have Arts Council and other subsidies, and it is difficult not to be dismayed that public money is spent to pay international celebrities brought for Puccini's and other popular operas which can be heard (with the same singers) on multiple recordings. Apart from *Dido and Aeneas*, one recalls only one attempt to mount Purcell at Covent Garden – a sumptuous one indeed of *The Fairy Queen* to designs by Oliver Messel. It was in the 1930s, a few years before the Second World War, and its expense, said to have been borne largely by C. B. Cochran and other private subscribers, accounts for its short run. The music was directed by Constant Lambert. This production came nearly ten years after a series of Cambridge University productions with which Dennis Arundell was associated, though their instigator was Professor Dent. For many these were a first eye-opener and ear-opener to the chief glories of Purcell's last years. Surely they teach us that, though we still cannot expect their realisation from the commercial and sub-sidised theatre (however grateful we are to hear the music when broadcast), nor apparently are gramophone companies competing in Purcell's 'operas', there are dozens of places, full of young and keen music-lovers and equipped with halls, small theatres or other suitable sites for the work, equipped also with musicologists and literary historians. These are the universities, colleges of music and other educational institutions.

One of them should have special mention. The University of Nottingham found opportunity rather than limitation in using its Great Hall. Ivor Keys was then Professor of Music, and Hugh Willat contributed special knowledge of the Stuart masque and Restoration theatre, as did Christine Pirie of scenery and costumes. A highly successful week's run of *King Arthur* in 1956 was followed by *The Fairy Queen* in 1959 and *Dioclesian* (with Dennis Arundell as producer) in 1963.

If we classified Purcell's music strictly by our chapter headings here, we should have to put many of his most popular songs, and some of the best-known dances and instrument pieces, under 'Theatre and Dramatic Music', though most of us who have known them since our young days would have to consult a reference book to ascertain the dramatic provenance. How many who sang 'I attempt from love's sickness to fly' at school knew anything of *The Indian Queen*? Who knew that splendid rondeau from Aphra Behn's *Abdelazer, or the Moor's Revenge* until Britten chose it for his 'Young Person's Guide to the Orchestra'? We shall therefore include any discussion of songs and dances outside the 'operas', and usually performed separately, in the final chapter.

The end of the previous chapter would have been more humiliating if, instead of asking who knew that rondeau before hearing Britten's piece, it had asked who could recognise and name the provenance of the extract quoted at Ex. 35. It is the second part of a dance, and it also comes from *Abdelazer*, as does the song 'Lucinda is bewitching fair'. Until he turned over a few pages (before writing this guide) the questioner could not have recognised the dance or the song as contributed to *Abdelazer*; yet since that play was produced in the last year of Purcell's life the music is of high quality. The truth is that much Purcell has yet to be brought to light, and much already discovered by the editors of the Purcell Society volumes has yet to become known and as popular as its quality deserves.

Ex.35

Purcell would have been only fifty-three if he had lived until Handel came to England. Until then, and even after, a limited number of his songs and dances remained popular – well enough known for Gay to use them in *The Beggar's Opera*. Since then, however, even after editions like those by Tippett and Bergmann, or Britten and Pears, our familiarity with Purcell's dances and songs has not greatly increased; for anthologies and separate printings have made their first choices from Playford's collections, chiefly *Orpheus Britannicus*, and from items in the 'operas' which one often wishes were heard only in the original contexts.

'Take away the stage, and nine-tenths of what is valuable in his music is lost', writes A. K. Holland.[1] Nine-tenths is a pardonably exaggerated fraction, but we may deplore with Holland the fact that Playford's issue of *A Collection of Ayres for the Theatre*, 1692, probably supervised by Mrs Purcell, contains so small a portion of the total output of Purcell's act-tunes and dances. These continued in eighteenth-century productions of plays by Dryden, Congreve and similar writers, and we hear little else from Purcell's instrumental theatre music except what comes in the 'operas'. Are we reluctant to assemble pieces that do not come from a single work? There are rival recordings of suites from *Les Indes Galantes* and we sometimes hear a suite from *The Fairy Queen*; but there is enough incidental music – overtures and curtain pieces, act-tunes and dances – from various sources to make several splendid Purcell suites.

The catalogue in *Grove* does not uphold Holland's assertion even if that 'nine-tenths' includes numbers in the 'operas'. The list headed 'Incidental Music and Songs for Plays' is considerably shorter than the one headed 'Songs with Continuo'. If we add 'Trios and Duets with Continuo' and 'Sacred Songs' to the solo airs in odes and 'operas' the grand total exceeds three hundred. That first list tells us that eighty Purcell songs (there may have been other contributors) are distributed among some forty-four plays – unevenly, for many a play has only one or two while others have eight; but let what is *not* revealed be manifest from a consideration of one play.

In his last year Purcell contributed to an adaptation from Beaumont and Fletcher called *Bonduca, or The British Heroine*. The title and theme (Britons versus invaders, though this time Romans, not Saxons) reminds us of *King Arthur or the British Worthy*, and the story of Boadicea ('Bonduca' to Beaumont and Fletcher) assisted by Caractacus (who must have risen from the dead!) leading the

[1] A. K. Holland: *Purcell: The English Musical Tradition*. Bell, London, 1932.

British stalwarts might well have been used for a Dryden 'opera'. The *Grove* list mentions three songs and no other music in *Bonduca* – 'Britons strike home', 'Hear, ye gods of Britain' and 'O lead me to some peaceful gloom', given in that order. In fact they are but the highlights of a scene set in a Druid temple. Several soloists in turn repeat the prayers of the Chief Druid (bass), and each is supported by a chorus, which also completes the invocations of two priestesses who sing to an accompaniment that includes two flutes. The sound of the trumpet then introduces a martial duet, and 'Britons strike home!' makes the stirring finale, so much more impressive as scored and given within the play than as recalled at Proms in Wood's 'Sea Songs'.

That scene, worthy of an opera, is described only so that we shall imagine the difference between music as realised in the theatre and as, rightly, catalogued. Even the single song named as within a play does not necessarily tell us that there was no other music, no chorus or instrumental contribution. On the other hand there may have been plenty of plays in which more than one song simply provided a change from spoken dialogue, as do the songs Shakespeare required from Feste in *Twelfth Night*. The list begins with eight songs for Nathaniel Lee's *Theodosius* in 1680, and their titles 'Ah! cruel bloody fate', 'Hail to the myrtle shade', 'Hark, behold the heavenly choir' and so on, suggest a greater dramatic contribution than the comment of the singers' words, as does the single song noted from Tate's adaptation of *Richard II* in 1681 – 'Retired from any mortal's sight'. On the other hand Purcell contributed eight songs to Durfey's *A Fool's Preferment, or The Three Dukes of Dunstable* in 1688. They include 'I sighed and I pined', 'I'll mount to yon blue coelum', 'I'll sail upon the dog-star' and 'There's nothing so fatal as woman'. These titles suggest no surrounding incidental music or recitatives, no impressive *scena* as from an opera; rather do we imagine them delivered, even when pathetic, simply to be enjoyed as songs encapsulating a passing mood, as in *The Beggar's Opera*.

We already know of two splendid instrumental pieces in *Abdelazer*, but the single song for that play, 'Lucinda is bewitching fair', is not part of a musical complex; nor are 'Come away, do not stay' and the supremely beautiful 'Music for awhile' in Dryden and Lee's *Oedipus* of 1692, the year in which Shadwell's *The Libertine* elicited what schools have made Purcell's best-known song, 'Nymphs and shepherds, come away' – unless 'Fairest isle' is even better known. We need not go right through the list to prove how many of Purcell's songs used at recitals were originally for the theatre. He was already a sick man when he contributed 'From rosy bowers' to Part III of Durfey's *Don Quixote*; he had already composed the songs in the previous two parts of the play.

Probably the most frequent encomium of Purcell is directed at his felicitous setting of the English language. The simile 'fits like a glove' springs to mind when the music is allied to straightforward songs like 'Man is for the woman made', or other bluff and sociable verses, as also to longer and gentler pieces like 'On the brow of Richmond Hill' or 'Nymphs and shepherds'; obviously, however, the glove is heavily stretched in the more florid and Italianate settings with long semiquaver runs and big interval-leaps. Yet even in them we might as well search for a needle in a haystack as for a phrase that failed to suit the idioms of English accent and pronunciation. The fact was much extolled in prefaces by John Playford (a good friend of English composers and himself no mean musician) and by his son Henry, who was associated with his father until the former's death in 1686. Henry then took over the business, being therefore responsible for *Orpheus Britannicus* and publications containing Purcell's later and best music. Let us note, however, that no professional musician would have been greatly impressed if Purcell's achievement had been merely that praised in Milton's sonnet to Henry Lawes – 'Harry, whose tuneful and well-measured song'. It had been Lawes' fortune to be asked to supply music for *Comus*, and though such a song as 'Sweet echo' is not to be despised, Milton's declaration that Lawes *first* taught' our native composers 'just note and accent' is nonsense. Moreover the setting of one's native language to music without falsifying its accent should be expected from the least gifted composition student.

The difference between Purcell (or Schubert or Fauré) and Henry Lawes lies not in the accurate treatment of language but in the fact that the language suggests a *musical* conception, not merely a setting to music, in the mind of a great composer; which Henry Lawes was not, though a worthy one. (His younger brother, William, had more talent, probably because he did not depend upon words but invented rhythms and textures for his instrumental consorts.) A parody may show the difference between merely fitting notes to words 'like a glove' and being inspired to fine melody on reading words and contemplating such images as they evoke. Presented with the words 'Fairest isle, all isles excelling', the minor composer, asked to set them for a good soloist, would introduce the florid run on the second syllable of 'excelling', and would certainly not give the second syllable of 'fairest' a longer note than the first. The mere setting might produce something like Ex. 36a; the quotation at Ex. 36b may not be insulting in view of the point to be considered.

Ex.36

Recitative does, of course, require that kind of setting which most nearly reflects an actor's declamation, as Lully knew when France would not accept the treatment of its language to an equivalent of Italian recitative. Lully's *vers mesuré*, produced after careful study of tragic actors, can seem to us a little slow and ponderous; Purcell's can go fast at one place and impressively slowly at another, and nearly always (with the harmony of the harpsichord) it has a tendency to glow into *arioso*. This is well illustrated in a piece which has become a favourite only in recent years – a complex of recitative, *arioso* and aria called 'The Blessed Virgin's Expostulation', dealing with Mary's anxiety at losing the boy Jesus during the family visit to the Temple. Quotation from this fine work, except at very great length, is hardly useful; nor, indeed, is much further reference to the wealth of Purcell's songs. To deal with them at all adequately demands a full study like Richard Capell's *Schubert's Songs*. Until such a study is undertaken the reader is referred to pages 160–71 of Westrup's *Purcell*, and also to the final chapter of that exemplary book. It has already been very heavily consulted for this Guide, which will merely paraphrase its final comments unless it takes the more honest course of boldly cribbing them.

Purcell's pre-eminent talent was for melody, albeit melody not successfully conceived or revised with imagination of its harmonic context; and that melodic gift is most appealing in his vocal line.

Despite all the advances of modern music, most listeners still prize the melodic gift above others and, especially in operas of today, long for declamation to glow into lyricism. Westrup therefore finishes his tribute by quoting the second quatrain of Gerard Manley Hopkins' sonnet on Purcell, containing the phrase 'It is the forgéd feature finds me', and adding 'Could anything better express the stubborn originality of a great artist?'

Purcell's Personality and Character

Plenty of writing by Purcell's contemporaries assures us that he was enormously admired as an artist. None *directly* testifies to the belief that he was liked as a man, yet we may adduce reasons for that belief from the very fact that documentary evidence gives us no grounds for doubting it. Purcell's was a London of diarists and gossips, who would have let us know if any eminent man were even eccentric, a 'character', let alone bibulous or licentious. Pupils of the splendid Blow reported that he was 'of blameless morals and benevolent temper, but not totally free from the imputation of pride'. Would they have missed any justified comments on Blow's greatest friend and disciple?

Portraits suggest that Purcell looked older than he was. Older men liked his company. Only Kneller's portrait, as Westrup rightly says, 'is that of an idealised youth', presented with the foppish chevelure and trappings we see in formal portraits of other Restoration personages. More convincing portraits, like the frontispiece to the *Sonatas of Three Parts*, show a plump but not corpulent man-about-town. Hawkins' suggestion that Purcell was a toper are unfounded, despite our noticing beneath the big eyes, large Roman nose and humorous mouth an incipient double chin. In so few years could an addictively bibulous musician have composed so much, so carefully, so neatly, and with such astounding assurance? Could so prominent a man have discharged his professional duties even *once* while 'under the influence' without eliciting comment or reproof?

In his time the supplying of music for tavern catches or ribald comedies was no indication either of personal depravity or an admiration of licence. Because nobody mentions 'our Orpheus' as in any way dissolute or unsociable we believe him to have been liked by musicians and others. One document has been eagerly quoted. It comes from one Anthony Aston and concerns Purcell's dealing with Jemmy Bowen, a fine treble who took solo parts in several of Purcell's works:

'Some of the Music [musicians] told him to grace and run a division in such a place. "O let him alone," said Mr. Purcell. "He will grace it more naturally than you or I can teach him."'

Easy-going or shrewd? Both. Do not those portraits convey a calm shrewdness? There, surely, we see the man who welcomes convivial company in the little leisure his commitments allowed, both because he liked conviviality and because it was sensible to know the tastes of those he delighted to delight. The few extravagant and unsociable (sometimes pitiable) creatures among the great artists do not warrant a belief that musical genius normally inhabits someone remote, introspective, fanatical or self-indulgent. We imagine that Purcell, like Mozart, enjoyed the pleasures of life (when there was a chance to refresh himself with them). Like Mozart, too, he was a family man at ease with his neighbours. Fortunately the time and place in which his genius became manifest did not make the idealistic pursuit of his art a handicap to the pursuit of his livelihood and creature comforts.

A Summary Biography

1659 Henry Purcell born, second son of Thomas Purcell, instrumentalist and singer. Pepys met Thomas Purcell and Locke as 'Masters of Music' before the decision to bring Charles II from exile. Thomas sang at Charles II's coronation and became a Gentleman of the Chapel Royal. Lacking records, we suppose Henry to have been born and baptised in his father's parish, Westminster, at some time in late summer or early autumn.

1669 Enrolled chorister in the Chapel Royal under Cooke, who was followed in 1672 by the travelled ex-chorister, Humfrey. Purcell composes anthems and songs before his voice breaks.

1673 Assistant to Hingston, keeper of royal instruments. On the death of Humfrey in the following year Blow (aged 26) is appointed Master of the Royal Choristers and becomes Purcell's mentor, both informally and by arranged tuition. Some of Purcell's songs are published.

1677 Composer in ordinary for the Consort of Violins, i.e. royal string orchestra.

1679 Organist of Westminster Abbey, where he had formerly been organ tuner and had copied organ parts.

1680 The Four-part String Fantasias; the first of Purcell's Welcome Songs and his first known theatre music – for Lee's *Theodosius*.

1681 Purcell marries Frances Peters. Several commissions for theatre music.

1682 Succeeds Lowe as one of the Chapel Royal organists. Death of Thomas Purcell and of Henry's short-lived first child.

1683 The Sonatas of III Parts. Ode for Princess Anne's marriage. Two odes for St Cecilia festivals. Follows Hingston as maker and curator of the king's organs. Chosen to play the Renatus Harris instrument at the coming competition between organ builders at the Temple Church.

1685 Death of Charles II. Coronation (April) of James II, music including Purcell's 'My heart is inditing'. Welcome Song after the suppression of Monmouth's rebellion.

1686 Welcome Song 'Ye Tuneful Muses'. Catches and duets in Book 2 of *The Pleasant Musical Companion*.

1687 Welcome Song for the king's birthday, 'Sound the Trumpet'. Elegy on the death of John Playford. Songs published in

The Theater of Music. Many anthems this year and the following year.

1689 Coronation of William III and Mary. Appointed to the 'King's Private Music'. *Dido and Aeneas* performed at Priest's school in Chelsea.

1690 Much theatre music, including that for *Dioclesian*, later published.

1691 Music for Dryden's *King Arthur* and the anonymous *The Gordian Knot Untied.*

1692 *The Fairy Queen.* Music for *The Libertine* and other plays. Ode, 'Hail, bright Cecilia', given at Stationers' Hall, Purcell singing counter-tenor solos.

1693 Queen's Birthday Ode 'Celebrate this festival'. Sacred songs published in Part 2 of *Harmonia Sacra*. Several secular songs published. Music for at least nine plays.

1694 Revision of Playford's *Introduction to the Skill of Musick*. Even more theatre music than in the previous year. *Te Deum and Jubilate in D* for St Cecilia's Day. Further publication of many songs.

1695 Music for Queen Mary's funeral. Two elegies on the Queen's death. Music for nine plays, including *Abdelazer* and *Bonduca*, but most notable in scale *The Tempest* and *The Indian Queen*. Purcell dies 21 November and is buried with great honour five days later in Westminster Abbey. The memorial tablet with the phrase 'gone to that Blessed Place where only his Harmony can be exceeded' is in the north aisle close to the organ.

Index of Main References